Workbook

T0392206

Melanie Starren

with Caroline Nixon and Michael Tomlinson

CAMBRIDGE
University Press

Map of the book

1 A song and a dance

My goal

Mission Complete!

I can have a simple conversation about a familiar topic. **5**

I can write an email stating preferences and making suggestions. **4**

I can find specific information in simple texts. **3**

I can find out and write about the life of a popular musician. **2**

I can understand about music when I read a text. **1**

And I need ...

To do this, I will ...

So I can ...

I want to practice ...

⊛ Diary

What I already know about music ...

What I have learned about music ...

1 Make five music words using the music notes.

1 _ _ _ _ _ 2 _ _ _ 3 _ _ _ _ _ _ _ 4 _ _ _ _ _ 5 _ _ _ _ _ _

2 🎧 5.02 Listen and read. Complete with the correct kind of music.

classical music   disco   folk   opera

1

I went to a concert at the Royal Albert Hall in London over the vacation. I don't usually enjoy listening to _____ because my mom plays it ALL THE TIME at home, and the concerts are all very long. But this was different. It was for kids and teenagers, so it was more relaxed. This time the concert only lasted for an hour. I think I might go again. Do you want to come with me?
Kamile

2

My sister, Lucia, is really into music from the 60s and 70s. I was looking through her old vinyl records last week and found this one. I know you prefer hip-hop, and I do, too, but I was actually pretty impressed with it. Listen first. Then tell me if _____ is for you!

Anna

3

I'm going to the Green Man Festival in Wales next week. I can't wait! I like _____ music, and there's so much at the Green Man Festival for people our age! Even though I usually hate camping, the facilities here are great!
Jaime

3 Read the texts again. Say *yes* or *no*.

1   The concert at the Royal Albert Hall was too long.

2   Anna's record is different from the music she usually likes.

3   Jaime is sleeping in a tent.

4   Andrea is a fan of opera.

4

ONLINE REVIEW

A lot of people like _____, but I can't understand a single word they say! The women's voices are too high, and the men's voices are far too low. I just want to understand the story!   *Andrea*

For each question, choose the correct answer.

1

Win a family ticket for the Madrid Jazz Festival. In 50 words, tell us why you want the tickets to this event. Note – the winner must have at least one person under 14 in their family.

What must you do in order to win the competition?

A   write about why you would like to go to the festival

B   write about why you have never been to the festival

C   write about which family member you want to take to the festival

2

Hey Joe,

Did you see David Bisbal on TV last night? He did an interview and performed his latest song. It may be online if you missed it. I know you like him!

Claire

Why has Claire sent this text message?

A   to tell Joe where he might possibly be able to see the show

B   to give Joe her opinion about last night's show

C   to see if Joe still likes the performer that she recently saw on TV

3

You must be in your seats 15 minutes before the performance begins. If you're late, you'll have to wait until the intermission. Refreshments are served during the intermission.

Which one of the answers below is true?

A   Food and drink are included.

B   You will miss the first half of the performance if you don't arrive 15 minutes early.

C   The door opens 15 minutes before the start of the show.

4

● ● ●

Maria, I've just seen our favorite music star shopping! At first, I didn't recognize Charlie Puth. But when I did, I asked if I could take a selfie of us, and he let me!

Santiago

Why has Santiago sent Maria this text message?

A   to tell Maria about an unusual event that happened to him

B   to check if Maria wants to see the picture he recently took of someone famous

C   to let Maria know about a special event where she can meet a star

2 **You've just seen your favorite singer.** Read the message and write your own.

Guess who I just saw? Pink! She was walking into a clothing store with her friends, and I opened the door for them. I recognized her immediately because of her hair. It's amazing! She said hi and thanks to me. She's really kind! I really admire her.

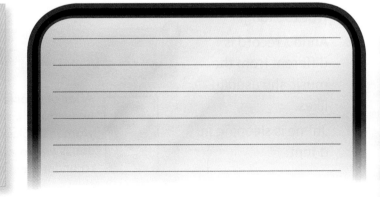

★ Grammar: adjectives with prepositions

1 **Complete the sentences with the correct preposition.**

> about   about   ~~for~~   in   of   of   on   with

1   David Guetta is famous ____for____ his songs with musicians like the Black Eyed Peas and Rihanna. He's also a successful DJ.

2   I'm not that interested _____ jazz, but I love disco.

3   She's tired _____ being in the studio all day. She'd rather see her fans!

4   Lucas was happy _____ being in the crowd when Shakira's car arrived.

5   He's afraid _____ photographers posting bad pictures of him online!

6   Our teacher looks bored _____ saying the same thing every day. Maybe we should do our homework on time.

7   Lily's very excited _____ meeting Calvin Harris. She's so lucky!

8   Thiago is focusing _____ classical music. He's been learning the violin since he was six.

2 ★ **Complete the text with the correct words.**

My sister Helen has always been interested ¹_____in_____ music. She can sing beautifully and plays the flute and the piano. She used to write songs for famous people to sing, but she got tired ²_____ that very quickly. She says she doesn't want to be famous ³_____ her music, and I know she's worried ⁴_____ people writing things about her online. She's interested ⁵_____ working with young people, but she doesn't want to be a teacher. So, she's decided to help people using music – doing music therapy in a hospital. When children are sick or scared, she works with them by playing music, dancing, and singing. She's very excited ⁶_____ her new job. She knows the beneficial effect of music and has always said that music is good ⁷_____ you!

3 **In pairs, talk about the pictures.** Use the adjectives and prepositions in Activity 1.

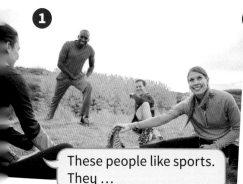

These people like sports. They …

1 Complete the descriptions with the correct adjectives.

If you could create your perfect friend, what would they be like?

For me, a perfect friend is someone I can have fun with. He or she should be ¹cheerful and happy most of the time, and he or she shouldn't be too ²s_____ or sensible. But he or she has to be ³r_____, too. If a friend is always late, even the funniest joke won't make me smile!

I'm lucky because my best friend, Martin, is perfect! He's ⁴i_____ and gets good grades in school. He's also ⁵p_____ and can explain things to me. When it's my birthday, he knows exactly what to buy me and is very ⁶g_____. My parents like him because he's polite and ⁷c_____. They are very fond of him. Sometimes, I think they like Martin more than me!

I don't think it's possible to have a perfect friend. I have three very good friends in school, and they are all perfect in different ways. Anna is good at sports, Sara is interested in the same things as me, and Marta is very kind. If you aren't ⁸r_____ or horrible to other people, and you don't tell us what to do (we can't stand ⁹b_____ people!), you can be our friend.

2 Read the school reports and answer the questions.

Selin is very intelligent and is always cheerful. Her exam scores this year were excellent, and I'm very happy with her progress. She can, though, be a little bossy and should try to be more patient.

| English | 97% | Math | 83% | History | 98% |

Emiliano has had a good year. He finds some subjects difficult, but he works hard. He's fantastic at sports, in particular tennis. He's a reliable and popular member of the class and can be very charming.

| English | 70% | Math | 84% | Science | 57% |

1 Who is better at math?

2 Who got the best exam scores overall this year?

3 Who would you prefer to be friends with? Why?

3 Write a school report for your friend using the adjectives in Activity 1.

_____
_____
_____
_____
_____

★ Grammar: short answers with *so* or *neither*

1 **Choose the correct answer.**

1   I love the soundtrack to the new *Sherlock Gnomes* movie. (So do I.) / Neither do I.

2   Richard didn't remember to bring his headphones to the gym. **So did Laura.** / **Neither did Laura.**

3   I would like to travel when I'm older. **Neither would I.** / **So would I.**

4   I'm not going to listen to the podcast. **Neither am I.** / **So am I.**

5   You swam really well at the competition this weekend. **So did you.** / **Neither did you.**

6   Catalina hasn't eaten her piece of cake yet. **So have I.** / **Neither have I.**

2 **5.03** **Listen to the conversations.** Then complete the sentences and write your answer.

1   I would rather be _____ than _____ . _____

2   I can't _____ a _____ to school. _____

3   I _____ _____ to space. _____

4   I _____ _____ to my party last year. _____

Speaking

3 **Watch Ezgi and Pablo do some speaking practice.** Answer the questions.

1   What question couldn't Pablo answer at first? What did the teacher do to help?

2   What topics are mentioned?

3   Who doesn't always answer the teacher's questions?

4 📝 **Now copy and plan your own answers to the questions.**

Tell us about what kind of music you like.

Do you have a favorite singer or pop group?

What do you like doing in your free time?

PRONUNCIATION TIP!
Some words can sound as if they are joined to the next word, like "do you – d'you," "going to – gonna." It's important to be aware of this.

5 ▶ **Watch again and complete the phrases.**

1   How _____ ?

2   Ezgi, _____ what kinds of music you like.

SPEAKING TIP! Listen carefully to the teacher's questions and make sure you answer what he or she is asking you.

1 **Read the sentences about the story.** Answer *yes*, *no*, or *don't know*. **Explain your answers.**

1 Julie and Ash aren't interested in pop music videos.   no

In the story it says, "What a great weekend. We spent hours lip-synching to pop music videos."

2 The competition takes place every Sunday.

3 Julie didn't have a good idea for a name for the band.

4 Julie says that each band sings its own songs.

5 Julie's dad doesn't like classical music.

6 Jasha doesn't win the competition.

2 **When Ash enters the band in the competition, Julie feels angry with her friend. Why? Discuss the three possible reasons (A–C) with a partner.**

A Julie thought Ash wasn't listening to her.

B Julie wanted to enter the band in the competition.

C Julie doesn't think the competition is very interesting.

3 **How does Ash help Julie at the community center?** Write your ideas below.

⭐ **Read this email from your English-speaking friend, Ash, and the notes you have made.**

Ask what time the concert starts

Me, too!

To:	
From:	Ash

Hi,

I'm so excited about Saturday! I can't believe we're doing the concert. I'm so glad you're coming. It's great that all our friends will be there.

Julie is coming to my house afterward. Would you like to come, too? We could watch a movie or sing along to some videos. Which would you Tell Ash ——prefer? Or would you like to do something else?

See you on Saturday (I hope!),

Ash

Suggest …

Write your email to Ash in about 100 words, using all your notes.

To:	
From:	

Remember to begin your email with a friendly phrase such as "It's great to hear from you" or "I was so happy to get your email."

Cross-curricular

1 Read the texts about Beethoven and Mozart again. Answer the questions.

1 Who were their first teachers?

Their first teachers were their fathers.

2 What were their first instruments?

3 What do you think their childhoods were like? Do you think they were happy and they had fun?

4 What kinds of problems did they have when they got older?

5 How old were they when they died?

6 How were their lives similar, and how were they different?

2 Read the text. How have DJs become popular?

Beethoven and Mozart's music was played for kings and important families around Europe. Today, we can all go to concerts or listen to our favorite music at home. Music continues to change, and house music is now very popular.

Not very long ago, pop singers and rock musicians were the kings and queens of music. Friends used to argue about the best band, and they saved up their allowance to buy their favorite bands' latest records. In the past, DJs simply played the music that the people asked for, but today they create the music. DJs have taken over pop culture, and they are quickly becoming the new celebrities. It began in the 1990s when house music became popular. Young people, who loved to dance, were more interested in the beat or rhythm of the song than the words. Technology has helped DJs develop this style of music. They can download the beat and the vocals and create new music easily. DJs are now as popular as the original musicians. They have thousands of fans who will travel across the country to watch them perform.

3 Find out and write about the life and music of a popular musician from your country.

Name	
Date and place of birth	
Profession	
Style of music	
Important work	

1 For each question, choose the correct answer.

1

NEEDED

DJs to play hip-hop music for regular customers. Should be over 18.
Friendly club with its own modern equipment.

☐ A   The club is looking for new customers.

☐ B   The club is asking DJs to bring their own equipment.

☐ C   The club is looking for DJs over a certain age.

2

Lorena,
Sorry if I was rude earlier. I hardly ever argue with friends. I was surprised that you didn't tell me about the dance party, that's all.
Call me when you get home.
Ashley

Ashley wants Lorena

☐ A   to be less rude.

☐ B   to contact her later.

☐ C   to tell her about the dance party.

3

Do not touch

Do not touch or pick up these instruments unless a museum officer is present.

Visitors to the museum

☐ A   are not allowed to hold the instruments.

☐ B   can only hold the instruments when a staff member is there.

☐ C   can ask a staff member to tell them about the instruments.

4

Kylie,
I finally met your drama teacher. He's not bossy. He was charming and patient! He told me which costume you need for the school show.

Mom   8:30

Kylie's drama teacher

☐ A   spoke to Kylie's mom about the school show.

☐ B   explained why he is so strict during drama classes.

☐ C   has a costume for Kylie.

5

Drinks, snacks, and hot food from the school cafeteria should not be taken into the hall or on the stage.

☐ A   If you are hungry, you can buy something in the hall.

☐ B   You can't eat or drink on the stage, but you can in the hall.

☐ C   You can't eat or drink anything in this area.

My progress: ☐ /5

1 🎧 5.04 **For each question, choose the correct answer.**

1 Which part of the girl's body was sore recently?

A ▢   B ▢   C ▢

2 What will the children do first?

A ▢   B ▢   C ▢

3 Who did the man send the video to first?

A ▢   B ▢   C ▢

4 Which article does Bridget always read?

A ▢   B ▢   C ▢

5 Which festival did the boy enjoy the most?

A ▢   B ▢   C ▢

6 Which activity did the girl manage to do by herself at summer camp?

A ▢   B ▢   C ▢

My progress: /6

1 Choose the correct answer.

1 I'm happy (about)/ of / for winning the prize.

2 Mario is great for / at / in baking cakes.

3 We're ready in / for / of the concert.

4 This raincoat is good for / at / about the rain.

5 Mom was proud with / for / of Lucy when she heard her sing.

6 Jaime isn't interested with / in / at hip-hop music.

2 Match the sentences (1–6) to the answers (A–F).

1 I wouldn't want to be an opera singer.

2 I'm not very good at sports.

3 I can't play a musical instrument.

4 Helen got 10/10 in English today.

5 Tristan and Zac have a rabbit.

6 I'll tell the teacher what happened.

A So do I.

B Nor can I.

C Nor would I.

D So will I.

E So did I.

F Nor am I.

3 Order the letters to make words. Complete the sentences.

| aoerp | ~~disuto~~ | iarellbe | lkfo | sugereon | sysbo |

1 Ariana Grande is in the ___studio___ recording a new song.

2 My sister is very _____ . She always tells me what to do.

3 The _____ music festival was great. There were lots of people with guitars.

4 I don't like _____ . I don't understand Italian, and I can't understand the story.

5 Uncle Lucas is very _____ . He buys me lots of presents.

6 James isn't _____ . He's always late, and he never does what he promises to do.

4 Complete the text with the correct answer.

| ~~cheerful~~ | good at | hip-hop | jazz | nor do we | opera | patient | so am I |

This is Mrs. Holt. She's my music teacher in school. I love her classes because she's really
[1] ___cheerful___ and [2]_____ explaining things. She's really into classical music, and [3]_____ .
She loves watching the performers sing as well as act. Her favorite instrument is the trumpet, like
me. She's always [4]_____ and positive in classes. We're preparing for
a concert right now. The members of the [5]_____ band are practicing
their trumpets, guitars, drums, and other instruments; the [6]_____
dancers are getting their performance ready; and Sally is singing
[7]_____ on stage. Everything is going well, but Mrs. Holt is looking a bit
serious. I know she doesn't want anything to go wrong when we're on stage,
and [8]_____ !

2 Big wide world

My goal

I can answer questions about celebrations. **5**

Mission Complete!

I can talk about and give personal information. **3**

I can read and understand information about countries around the world. **4**

I can listen and complete a text with specific information. **1**

I can read and understand important information about our planet in a text. **2**

And I need ...

To do this, I will ...

So I can ...

I want to practice ...

⊛ Diary

What I already know about the world around us ...

_____

_____

What I have learned about the world around us ...

_____

_____

1 **Look at the shapes and write the names of the continents.**

1 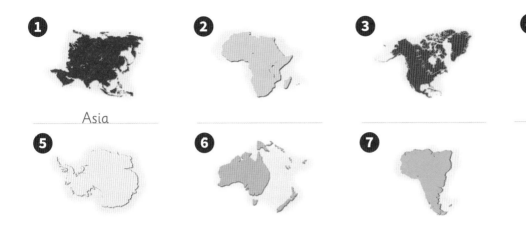 Asia

2

3

4

5

6

7

2 🎧 5.05 **Read and complete the facts.** Then listen and check.

1 The flag of _____China_____ is yellow and _____ .

2 The border between the U.S.A. and _____ is the longest in the world.

3 The capital of _____ isn't Sydney; it's Canberra.

4 _____ is made up of England, Northern Ireland, Scotland, and Wales.

5 Turkey is on two continents: Asia and _____ .

6 _____ , which is also called Éire, celebrates St. Patrick's Day.

3 **Read the information and fill in the blanks.**

There are over **7,000** [1]l_____ in the world. There are 2,301 spoken in Asia alone!

People of many [2]n_____ live in the U.S.A. Around **50 million** people who live there **aren't** American.

The Earth has a very varied [3]c_____ . Here are some **world records**. The hottest temperature: 56.7˚C. The coldest temperature: -89.2˚C.

Planet Earth has a diverse [4]l_____ , but only 43% is habitable. There are lots of different [5]c_____ in the world, and the diversity on our planet is amazing!

1 🎧 5.06 **You will hear a boy named Oliver talking about a trip he took with his family. Put the pictures in the correct order.**

A

B [1]

C

D

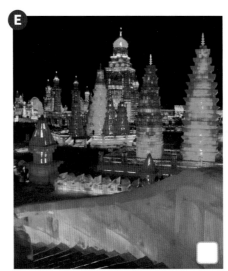

E

F

2 🎧 5.07 ⭐ **Listen again. For each question, write the correct answer in the blank. Write one or two words.**

The family's trip was planned by Oliver's ¹ _____sister_____ .

Oliver was surprised to see how popular ² _____ was in Moscow.

Oliver and his family traveled from Russia to China by ³ _____ .

Oliver says there were around ⁴ _____ pandas at the wildlife park in Chengdu.

Oliver found it hard to get used to the ⁵ _____ in Morocco.

When he's older, Oliver would like to visit the ⁶ _____ in Morocco.

Grammar: relative clauses

1 **Complete with *who*, *which*, *whose*, or *where*. Check (✓) the sentences where *that* is also correct.**

1 I wore the blue bathing suit. You gave it to me for my birthday.

I wore the blue bathing suit _____ you gave me for my birthday. ☐

2 Chris Hemsworth is an actor. He comes from Australia.

Chris Hemsworth is an actor _____ comes from Australia. ☐

3 We stayed in the hotel. A famous chef works there.

We stayed in the hotel _____ the famous chef works. ☐

4 Thomas was speaking to the man. His daughter made the moon cakes.

Thomas was speaking to the man _____ daughter made the moon cakes. ☐

2 **Complete the non-defining relative clauses. Use *which*, *where*, or *whose*.**

1 James can explain the story of the dragon dance. (His mom comes from Shanghai.)

James, _____ , can explain the story of the dragon dance.

2 Grace speaks Swahili. (It's spoken by over 100 million people.)

Grace speaks Swahili, _____ .

3 Brazil is the largest country in South America. (Portuguese is spoken there.)

Brazil, _____ , is the largest country in South America.

3 **Match the sentence halves (1–6) to their endings (A–F). Then complete with *who*, *which*, *whose*, or *where*.**

1 The glass slipper was the object
2 Hagrid is the giant
3 Camp Nou is the stadium
4 This is Andy Murray,
5 J.R.R. Tolkien is the author
6 They speak Spanish,

A _____ brother is also a tennis player.
B _____ is spoken by over 400 million people!
C ___which___ Cinderella lost at midnight.
D _____ wrote *The Hobbit*.
E _____ brother is named Grawp.
F _____ the Barcelona soccer team plays.

4 **In pairs, say defining and non-defining sentences about the following pictures.**

Paris, where the Eiffel Tower is, is …

Paris / capital city / Eiffel Tower

The White House / President of the U.S.A.

Ed Sheeran / guitar

Koke / Atlético Madrid

1 **Complete the ads with "place" words.**

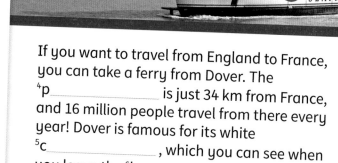

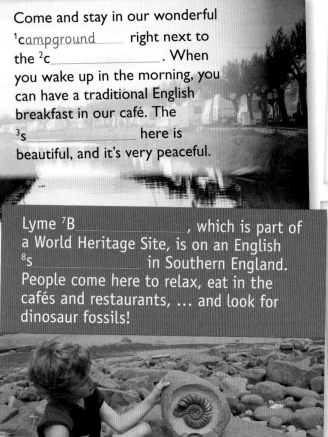

Come and stay in our wonderful
¹campground_____ right next to
the ²c_____. When
you wake up in the morning, you
can have a traditional English
breakfast in our café. The
³s_____ here is
beautiful, and it's very peaceful.

If you want to travel from England to France,
you can take a ferry from Dover. The
⁴p_____ is just 34 km from France,
and 16 million people travel from there every
year! Dover is famous for its white
⁵c_____, which you can see when
you leave the ⁶h_____.

Lyme ⁷B_____, which is part of
a World Heritage Site, is on an English
⁸s_____ in Southern England.
People come here to relax, eat in the
cafés and restaurants, ... and look for
dinosaur fossils!

Our canoeing center is
in a beautiful Welsh
⁹v_____.
Just push your canoe
into the river, jump in,
and paddle happily
down the River Wye.
Perfect for beginners
and experts.

2 **Look and complete the mind maps.** In pairs, compare your ideas.

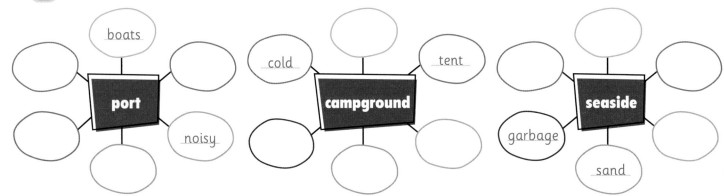

boats — **port** — noisy

cold — **campground** — tent

seaside — garbage — sand

3 **In pairs, choose and describe one of the pictures.** Use the words in Activity 2, or
your own ideas.

This is a picture of ...

It looks ...

It might be ...

★ **Grammar:** *more ... than, fewer ... than, less ... than, the most, the fewest, the least*

1 **Choose the correct answer.**

1 There are **less** / **fewer** countries in South America than in Europe.
2 Sandra speaks **more** / **the most** languages than anyone I know. She's amazing!
3 She got **the fewest** / **the least** points in the geography tests. She was very upset.
4 There's **few** / **less** noise at the campground at night than during the day.
5 Money is **the least** / **fewest** important thing for me.
6 She is **the most** / **more** well-traveled person in my family. She's been everywhere!

2 **Write sentences with the words in the box.**

fewer   less   the fewest   the least

1 Natalia has _____ cards than Thiago.

2 Felipe has _____ cards.

3 Simba has _____ space than Rory.

4 Paws has _____ space.

Speaking

3 ▶ **Watch Ezgi do some speaking practice.** Listen and number the words in order.

A at the front ☐   C on the left ☐

B in the middle ☐   D at the back ☐

4 **In pairs, take turns to describe these things without saying the word.**

cash machine   helmet   horror movie
mouse   port   rude   sneakers

SPEAKING TIP! If you don't know the word for something, try describing it, or saying what it isn't.

5 ▶ **Imagine you're Pablo. Describe your picture. Then listen to Pablo.**

It's a / They're a type of ...

It isn't / They aren't ...

6 ▶ **Watch again and write four phrases to give you time to think.**

1 _____   3 _____

2 _____   4 _____

1 **Answer the questions.**

1 What is the importance of colored powder in the Holi Festival?
The colored powder makes everyone look the same.

2 Why is the Holi Festival celebrated in so many different parts of the world?

3 Why is the festival in Thailand called the Monkey Buffet?

4 What is the importance of monkeys to the people of Thailand?

5 What do the people of Sumpango spend a lot of their free time doing?

6 What do the messages on the kites tell us about the people of Sumpango?

2 **Complete the article with the words from the box.**

celebrates explodes festival festivities new ~~population~~

The Chinese New Year, or Spring Festival, is celebrated in Chinese communities in many different countries all over the world. One-sixth of the ¹_____population_____ of the world ²_____ the Chinese New Year. The ³_____ starts on the first day of the ⁴_____ moon, which is always on one of the last ten days of January, or on one of the first 20 days of February. People decorate the streets with red lanterns. The sky ⁵_____ with the light from thousands of fireworks, and children wear new clothes, and receive red envelopes containing gifts of money from their parents, grandparents, uncles, and aunts. Every Chinese New Year is named after a different animal (the Year of the Ox, the Year of the Dragon, the Year of the Pig, etc). The ⁶_____ last for 15 days.

3 ⭐ **For each question, choose the correct answer.** You will hear a radio interview about a festival.

1   The Spring Festival
    A   started last year.
    B   is new this year.
    C   is an annual event.

2   Last year everyone
    A   carried flowers.
    B   wore flower costumes.
    C   painted flowers on the floats.

3   The Spring Queen
    A   caught a bad cold.
    B   loved the flowers.
    C   had a problem with the flowers.

4   School children
    A   played with the brass band last year.
    B   are playing the music at the parade this year.
    C   are marching to the music of the brass band this year.

5   There
    A   are going to be cakes and sandwiches to eat.
    B   are going to be pies for everyone to eat.
    C   isn't going to be any food at the festival this year.

6   The puppet shows
    A   were very popular last year.
    B   are going to be held in the town hall.
    C   are new this year.

1 Match the sentence halves (1–5) to their endings (A–E).

1 Ocean plants
2 If the ocean gets too warm,
3 Krill like to live
4 Sea turtles and many kinds of fish
5 Algae

A in very cold water close to sea ice.
B live in coral reefs.
C make their own food, like plants.
D many plants and animals will have to adapt or die.
E take in a quarter of the carbon dioxide we produce.

2 Read the text and answer the questions.

Scientists around the world have become very worried because the level of the ocean is getting higher. If the levels continue to go up, this will be a serious problem for places that are close to the sea. Why is this happening? Earth is getting warmer because we produce a lot of carbon dioxide.

This gas stops the heat from Earth escaping back into space. As a result, Earth's ice is melting, and the level of the ocean is rising because of the extra water. We need to reduce the amount of carbon dioxide that we produce, before it is too late.

Plants use carbon dioxide to make their food, so we should also protect the forests and plant more trees. We should also stop using coal and oil to produce energy, and start using alternative energy like solar and wind energy.

1 Why is the level of the ocean getting higher?

_____

2 Why is Earth's ice melting?

_____

3 Why is the Earth's temperature increasing?

_____

4 Why should we plant more trees?

_____

5 What do you think will happen if the level of the oceans continues to get higher?

_____

3 Find out and complete the chart.

	Pacific Ocean	Indian Ocean	Arctic Ocean	Atlantic Ocean	Southern Ocean
How big is it?				106,500,000 km^2	
How deep is it?				3,339 m	

1 **Work in groups of three: one teacher and two students, A and B.**

A and B: close your books. Speak for 2–3 minutes.

Teacher: ask questions.

Teacher

Student A   Student B

2 **First, ask their name, age, and where they live.**

Good morning/ afternoon, how are you?

A

What's your name? (pause) How old are you? (pause) Thank you.

Where do you live? (pause) Who do you live with? (pause) Thank you.

What's your name? (pause) How old are you? (pause) Thank you.

B

Where do you live? (pause) Who do you live with? (pause) Thank you.

3 **Then, ask about everyday routines or situations.** Choose up to four questions each.

Tell us about a country you've visited.

What's your favorite subject in school?

How do you prefer to travel?

What kind of music do you like listening to?

Tell us about a language you would like to learn.

How often do you travel by car?

How do you spend your time on weekends?

Which do you like best, hot or cold weather?

Thank you.

My progress:

I understood and answered all the questions. ☐	I understood and answered most of the questions. ☐	I didn't understand all the questions and needed some help. ☐

1 **Five sentences have been removed from the article.** For each blank, choose the correct sentence. There are three extra sentences which you do not need to use.

European Life

I was born in China, Beijing, the capital city. I went to the same school in the center of the city until I was ten. ¹☐ One day, when I got home, my parents said they had something serious to tell me. My first thought was that they had heard I was getting terrible grades.

²☐ In fact, they told me that we had a new home in Europe! I had only seen places like France and Portugal on a map, and I had no idea what life would be like so far away. The more we talked about it, the more curious I became. The country was Austria, and so I contacted a cousin who lived in Vienna to ask him some questions. About a week later, he emailed me some pictures and a description of his daily life. They made me realize how different life there was compared with China. ³☐

When the airplane landed, I felt sure we had done the wrong thing. I was already missing my friends. ⁴☐. I was learning to speak German as well as English. Fortunately, my grades were improving. I didn't feel so lonely, I just felt lucky.

The truth is that I like my life more in Europe because it's easier to get to places like Italy, Greece, and Spain for fantastic vacations. A lot of my Chinese friends have visited me, too. Now I'm in my last year of school, so I'm preparing to go to a university in the U.K. ⁵☐ I'm so glad my parents decided to move here. Even if some of the food is totally different from Beijing, I still look forward to visiting China to eat my favorite dishes at New Year. I can see my friends and visit my grandma then, too!

A   It was nothing about my progress in class.

B   However, a week later I had met a bunch of new people in a large international school.

C   I was never very good at math and English.

D   I'm planning to study business when I'm there.

E   It was a small building with cheerful and patient teachers.

F   I can still remember my ninth birthday.

G   I couldn't imagine our modern apartment.

H   If he could deal with such a big change, then so could I.

My progress: ☐/5

1 Look at the pictures and complete the story with the missing phrases.

One sunny day, my parents and I were packing our car, ¹_____. We were really excited because we were going to stay by the seaside, ²_____. We had bought a new tent, too! When Mom and I were getting into the car, Dad stopped to speak to the woman ³_____. We were late so, in a hurry, we drove off. We didn't hear the key ⁴_____ fall on the ground. We arrived at the campsite late at night and wanted to put the tent up. My parents, ⁵_____ weren't happy when they realized they had lost the key. And the tent was in the box, too! But I still had Tony, my bear, so it wasn't a total disaster.

A   who lived next door

B   whose suitcases were in the box,

C   which had a box on the roof

D   where we had booked a nice campsite

E   which opened the box

2 Look at the facts. Then complete the sentences.

Continent	Number of countries	Percentage of Earth
Africa	54	20%
Asia	48	30%
Europe	46	7%
North America	4	16.5%
South America	13	12%

1   There are _____fewer_____ countries in North America than in South America.

2   There are _____ countries in Asia than in Europe.

3   The continent with _____ space is Europe.

4   The continent with _____ countries is Africa.

5   South America has _____ space than North America.

6   North America has _____ countries in the chart.

3 In pairs, say and guess the words. Use defining or non-defining relative clauses.

Antarctica   Australia   bay   campground climate   nationality   port   scenery   valley

This is a word that describes where you are from.

Review ••• Units 1–2

1 **Match the sentence halves (1–6) to their endings (A–F).**

1 Grace is good at ——————— A who comes from Australia.
2 They are the scientists who ——— B playing the drums.
3 I was speaking to someone   C is the amazing variety of culture.
4 There are fewer   D of singing on stage.
5 Lucia is scared   E are studying the penguins.
6 The best thing about Asia   F than 25,000 polar bears in the wild.

2 **Complete the sentences.**

1 I'm happy ___about___ going on a trip to the mountains.

2 There are more people in the capital city _____ in my town.

3 "I've been to North America twice." "So _____ I! The U.S.A. and Canada."

4 Jinpin, _____ sells secondhand clothes in our town, is always very cheerful.

5 Jim is my friend _____ little brother is annoying.

6 Jim is patient _____ his little brother.

3 📝 👁 **Find the mistake in each sentence.** **Re-write the sentences correctly.**

1 Africa is an amazing continent which you can see wild animals and beautiful scenery.

   Africa is an amazing continent where you can see wild animals and beautiful scenery.

2 I most like rock music.

   _____

3 I like best the coast.

   _____

4 A DJ is a person plays music.

   _____

5 My sister is more happier than my brother.

   _____

6 The mountain areas are cold than the forest.

   _____

4 **Order the letters.** **Label the pictures.**

drue
gatse
gdarmpocun
cotsa

1 **Look at the instructions. Think about a story.**

- Your English teacher has asked you to write a story.
- Your story must begin with this sentence:

  My parents both looked really excited when they gave me the envelope at breakfast.

2 **Read Kamile's story.**

My parents both looked really excited when they gave me the envelope at breakfast. Inside was a birthday card with a picture of a piece of old rock. I was surprised because it was an unusual choice of card for me. When I opened the card, a recording of some American music played. My mom laughed at how confused I looked and gave me some new hiking boots. "Can you guess where we're going?" she asked. Then it all became clear. "The Grand Canyon!" I cried. It was the best birthday surprise ever.

3 **Which three adjectives does Kamile use to show emotions?**

It's a good idea to think about how the main characters show how they feel.

4 **Complete the sentences with the words in the box.**

amazed   cheerful   surprised   terrified

1   I was so _____ of swimming with sharks that I cried every night for a week before we left.

2   Matthew's usually a very _____ person, and he is always smiling.

3   Jess didn't expect to see Martin there and was so _____ she couldn't speak.

4   My mom was so _____ when she heard they were getting married that she bought them a present.

5 **Now do the task in Activity 1. Use adjectives to say how your characters were feeling. Write your story in about 100 words.**

3 Shopping around

Mission Complete!

My goal

I can write a simple story. ★5

I can decide if sentences are true or false. ★3

I can give my opinion and agree or disagree on a given topic. ★4

I can understand a listening text. ★1

I can talk about things I did in the past related to shopping. ★2

And I need ...

To do this, I will ...

So I can ...

I want to practice ...

Diary

What I already know about shopping ...

What I have learned about shopping ...

③

1 Find the words and complete the definitions.

1 how much something costs ___price___
2 something that is cheaper than normal
   _____
3 something plastic you use to buy something now and pay later _____
4 a piece of paper to show you have paid for something _____
5 a piece of paper asking for payment
   _____
6 someone who helps customers _____
7 money you get back if you gave more than necessary _____
8 notes and coins, but not cards _____

S	A	I	R	P	W	Y	E	L
A	P	B	A	R	G	A	I	N
L	H	O	T	B	T	S	K	S
E	R	I	W	Y	O	C	Q	D
S	E	E	E	S	D	R	Y	O
C	C	H	A	N	G	E	W	B
L	E	B	N	E	W	D	B	I
E	I	S	S	M	R	I	A	L
R	P	R	I	C	E	T	H	L
K	T	G	E	C	H	C	W	K
M	A	Z	Y	C	P	A	E	P
N	J	C	A	S	H	R	Y	U
T	O	I	O	V	R	D	U	X

(PRICE is circled)

2 Look at the exchange rates and the pictures. Complete the receipts.

EXCHANGE RATES
For £1, you can buy …

country	currency	rate
Europe	EUR	1.15
U.S.A.	USD	1.5
Australia	AUD	1.7

 £1.25

 £10

 £20

THANK YOU FOR YOUR PURCHASE
- - - - - - - - - - - - - - - - - - -
2 x magnets
1 x hoodie (L)
1 £ _____
paid in U.S. dollars = **2** $ _____
cash $40
change **3** $ _____

PLEASE CALL AGAIN!
- - - - - - - - - - - - - - - - - - -
1 x teddy bear
1 x Big Ben statue
4 £ _____
paid in EUR = **5** € _____
cash 20€
change **6** € _____

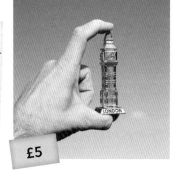 £5

3 You have 20 Australian dollars. In pairs, talk about what you'd like to buy.

Australia	AUD	1.7

I'd like to buy …

1 Find someone who ...

paid a very high price for something. _____

got something for a bargain. _____

paid for something by credit card. _____

bought something yesterday. _____

bought something they didn't need. _____

bought something they regret. _____

tried to change something but didn't have the receipt. _____

bought something using dollars. _____

2 Read the text below and choose the correct word for each blank.

A bank that deals with cheese

To most people, Parmesan cheese is just a delicious cheese to have with pasta. However, some Italians [1]_____ it to be as valuable as gold.

If that sounds [2]_____ , then think about how much cheese Italy actually produces. It's the biggest cheese producer in the world, and Parmesan is one of its most popular cheeses. Since Parmesan takes two years before it's ready to eat, cheesemakers often experience financial [3]_____ before it's ready to sell and can't afford to buy ingredients to make more cheese.

Since 1953, the Credito Emiliano bank has [4]_____ cheesemakers to bring in their Parmesan cheese wheels to get loans. The bank keeps the cheese in specially built rooms until a cheesemaker has [5]_____ back the loan.

This unusual Italian bank has been a great [6]_____ in helping cheesemakers grow their business while the bank takes care of their Parmesan cheese that's worth its weight in gold.

1	A respect	B consider	C feel	D recognize
2	A unforgettable	B hopeless	C challenging	D impossible
3	A difficulties	B effects	C situations	D disadvantages
4	A accepted	B applied	C allowed	D admitted
5	A put	B paid	C taken	D sent
6	A effort	B gain	C progress	D success

Grammar: verb + gerund, verb + infinitive

1 Choose the correct answer.

1 Lucas wants (to buy) / buying something for his sister's birthday.

2 Alba didn't promise **to sell** / **selling** me her bike.

3 Fiona and I want **to watch** / **watching** something at the movies tonight.

4 Asil doesn't mind **to do** / **doing** the dishes.

5 We plan **to travel** / **traveling** around Asia next year.

6 My mom gave up **to learn** / **learning** to drive when she went around the traffic circle the wrong way!

2 Complete the text with the correct form of the verbs.

be   be   buy   get   hit   ~~watch~~   watch   win

I love ¹ ___watching___ tennis, and one day I would like ² _____ as good as Nadal! When I was in my first year in this school, I asked ³ _____ on the school team. Last year, I lost one of my games, but won ten. This year, I hope ⁴ _____ them all! I love being outdoors, and I practice ⁵ _____ the ball over the net and before the line hundreds of times a day, but I hate ⁶ _____ up early for my tennis lessons. I love ⁷ _____ people like Federer and Kyrgios play, but tickets to tennis games are very expensive. My dad always agrees ⁸ _____ tickets for us, since we're both big tennis fans!

3 Write sentences using one word from each column.

imagine	write	chocolate cupcake for breakfast
finish	wear	trumpet
fancy	get	letter to Santa
learn	be	mouse costume
need	play	100%
fail	eat	unicorn

4 In pairs, compare your sentences from Activity 3. Whose are the most interesting?

My first sentence is "Can you imagine being a unicorn?"

I said "I finished writing a letter to Santa." I prefer your sentence.

1 Read and complete with the words in the box.

cost   damaged   exchange   for sale   luxury   marked down
reasonable   return   sale   ~~secondhand~~   sold   spend

When I was younger, my family didn't have much money, but we were very happy. This is me at my first dance class. My shoes were ¹ ___secondhand___ and very dirty. They used to belong to my sister, but they were a little ² _____ at the front.

We usually shopped in thrift stores when I was little, but occasionally we bought clothes in the ³ _____. I remember my mom buying me this dress for my birthday. I think it was ⁴ _____.

The problem with buying things on sale is that sometimes you can't ⁵ _____ them for something else, or ⁶ _____ them

to get your money back. My grandparents are very generous with their grandchildren. They bought these jeans for my brother, but he didn't try them on first. He looks very silly!

When I was 13, my mom got a new job, and we had more money. Suddenly, we were able to ⁷ _____ more money on things we liked. We found a beautiful house that was ⁸ _____, so we ⁹ _____ our old one. We went on vacations abroad every year and stayed in ¹⁰ _____ hotels. I'm not sure how much the vacations ¹¹ _____, but we had lots of fun. We stayed in this hotel in India. It's beautiful, isn't it?

My favorite possession is a bracelet I bought last year. It looks really expensive, but it was pretty ¹² _____.

2 🎧 5.09 Listen to the conversations. Read and check (✓) the correct sentence.

1 A The sales clerk is going to exchange the laptop. ☐
   B The boy doesn't have a receipt for the laptop. ☐

2 A Hannah thinks the price is reasonable. ☐
   B Cara doesn't think the boots cost too much. ☐

3 A The guitar is cheap because it was damaged. ☐
   B The guitar is cheap because it isn't new. ☐

4 A The girl can exchange the little dog if he isn't friendly. ☐
   B The girl can't buy the dog she wants. ☐

★ **Grammar:** gerunds as subjects and objects

1 **Complete the sentences with the correct form of the verb in the box.**

> eat   have   look   ~~play~~   shop   swim

1   __Playing__ computer games every day is boring.

2   Lucia isn't happy about _____ a test on her birthday.

3   _____ on Saturdays is my sister's favorite hobby. She always buys a lot!

4   _____ fruit for breakfast is a good idea.

5   _____ for bargains in stores is a way of saving money.

6   I'm not interested in _____. because I hate getting wet .

2 **In pairs, order the words to make sentences.**

1   about   The best   riding   is that   a bike   thing   quickly.   you can get home

2   thing about   is that   doing the dishes   too busy to help.   The worst   my sister is always

3   Japan   when I'm older.   visit   I want to

4   doing   a good idea!   Not   for Mr. Thomas   your homework   is not

5   a movie   a good suggestion.   tonight   Watching   is

Speaking

3 ▶ **Watch Ezgi and Pablo do some speaking practice.** Complete the chart.

Agreeing	Disagreeing	Giving your own opinion
agree		

4 **Look at the pictures again and discuss the five ideas.** Which one would you choose?

5 ▶ **Watch again and <u>underline</u> which word or syllable is stressed in each phrase in Activity 3.**

PRONUNCIATION TIP! The tone of your voice is important, so be aware how you sound when discussing things.

SPEAKING TIP! Use different phrases to express your opinion. Always remember to be polite.

1 What is the main idea of the story? Choose the correct answer.

A It is about people who follow banknotes.

B It is about the journey of a banknote.

C It is about valuing a gift you get.

2 What journey did the banknote take? Look and draw lines.

3 Read the sentences. Answer *yes* or *no*.

1 Lincoln was a famous politician. _____yes_____

2 Lincoln was born on November 30, 1874. _____

3 Banknotes with unusual serial numbers are sometimes valuable. _____

4 Tom's dad liked to collect banknotes when he was a boy. _____

5 Tom bought the five-dollar bill online. _____

6 Tom now collects unusual banknotes. _____

4 Match the words from the text (1–6) to their meanings (A–F).

1 valuable   A to connect to a computer system

2 log in   B to pause

3 look at   C worth a lot of money

4 calmly   D to become visible

5 appear   E think about something carefully

6 take a deep breath F quietly, peacefully

5 **Read the ad and the example.** Then answer the questions.

ARTICLES WANTED FOR SCHOOL MAGAZINE!

My Allowance

How much allowance do you get?
What do you like to spend your money on?
Do you buy secondhand things?
Do you always look for a bargain?
Do you save any money?

We will print the most interesting and funny answers in the school magazine. Email stories to asimpson@grimmcollege.com

---

How I spend my allowance!

My mom and dad give me five dollars allowance every week if I do all my homework and keep my room neat. I get extra if I do the dishes.

I am pretty responsible, so the first thing I do is divide it in half. I take one half to school and spend it in the school store. Sometimes I buy a sandwich or a drink. The other half I save for special things – for example, if I want a new video game, music, clothes, or to go to the movies with my friends. When I get money on my birthday or at Christmas, I save it, too.

I love spending my allowance, but I love saving part of it, too.

---

1 What does the first paragraph talk about? _____
2 What does the second paragraph talk about? _____
3 What does the last sentence talk about? _____

6 **Use the following tips and write your article in about 100 words.**

- Write a title
- Say how much allowance you get and why
- Say what you spend it on
- Say how you feel about what you do with your allowance

1 **Match the sentence halves (1–5) to their endings (A–E).**

1 The goldsmith gave the owner   A   you could exchange items.

2 In the 1950s, credit cards   B   in China to pay for things.

3 Shells were used   C   a receipt for the gold.

4 Bartering meant that   D   and difficult to carry.

5 Gold was heavy   E   were invented.

2 **What would you exchange for these things?** Choose from the pictures.

1 a pair of jeans

2 a candy bar

3 a comic book or magazine

4 a basketball or soccer ball

5 a banana

3 **Write about your country's money.**

1 What is it called? _____

2 Which coins does it use? _____

3 Which banknotes does it use? _____

4 What is the smallest coin, and what is the largest banknote? _____

5 Where is the money made? _____

4 **Design a banknote for your class.**

Remember:
Banknotes are made on special paper. They have complicated patterns to stop copying.

They have a secret line called a watermark.
Write the value on the banknote.

1 Work in groups of three: one teacher and two students, A and B.

A and B: listen to the teacher and then speak for 2–3 minutes.

Teacher: read and then listen to A and B speak. Use a timer.

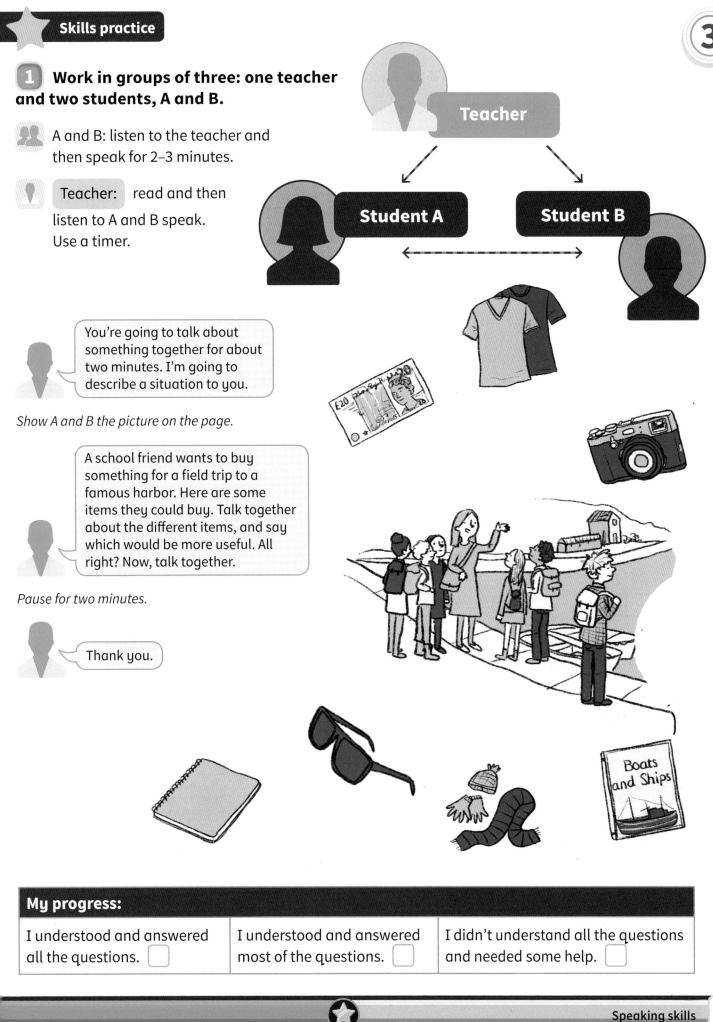

Teacher

Student A ⟷ Student B

> You're going to talk about something together for about two minutes. I'm going to describe a situation to you.

Show A and B the picture on the page.

> A school friend wants to buy something for a field trip to a famous harbor. Here are some items they could buy. Talk together about the different items, and say which would be more useful. All right? Now, talk together.

Pause for two minutes.

> Thank you.

My progress:		
I understood and answered all the questions. ☐	I understood and answered most of the questions. ☐	I didn't understand all the questions and needed some help. ☐

1 **Read the text. Write <u>one</u> word for each blank.**

Write your answers in **CAPITAL LETTERS** below the text.

My favorite market

I love to look for bargains at the secondhand market in my town. I've saved loads of
money by shopping there. That means I can spend the rest of my allowance on other
things, such ¹… going out with my friends! The market is always busy because it's in
the center ²… town, in a really nice area along the canal. Every day, there are ³…
least 50 different stands that sell various used goods.

When I want to buy some secondhand designer clothes, I'll see what's at the market.
I know the best time to get the best deals on clothes ⁴… before nine o'clock. That's
because the ⁵… reasonable items are always sold by noon! After I finish shopping,
I'll often go to a popular café next to the market, where I can get a sandwich and
coffee for less ⁶… $5.

---

1 ☐☐☐☐☐

2 ☐☐☐☐☐

3 ☐☐☐☐☐

4 ☐☐☐☐☐

5 ☐☐☐☐☐

6 ☐☐☐☐☐

My progress: ☐ /6

(3)

1 Complete the sentences with the correct form of the verb.

~~buy~~   not put   play   return   speak   visit

1 Iker would like _____to buy_____ a luxury house with a soccer field.

2 Yuck! My sister promised _____ jelly in my shoes, but look!

3 My puppy loves _____ with my socks.

4 Martina doesn't mind _____ her elderly neighbor every Sunday. He bakes delicious cupcakes!

5 I agreed _____ Noa's library books.

6 Kim and I wanted _____ to our P.E. teacher after school, but she was too busy.

2 Complete the sentences with the correct form of the verbs in parentheses.

1 _____Watching_____ movies and _____ hot chocolate is my favorite activity when it's cold and raining. (watch / drink)

2 _____ is fun if you have a good bike and don't mind going up hills! (ride your bike)

3 I'm not happy about _____ the dishes again. It's your turn! (do)

4 Not _____ your change before leaving a store is a bad idea. (check)

5 _____ a tie to my party isn't necessary. (wear)

6 I enjoy _____ to the park with my friends to hang out on weekends. (go)

3 Complete the sentences.

1 I need a size 5. I'll ask the _____sales_____ clerk.

2 Here's your change and your r_____ .

3 My new smartphone wasn't too expensive. It was actually pretty r_____ .

4 Last week, this skirt cost $22, but yesterday it was m_____ to $11 on sale.

5 How many e_____ does a train ticket from Huelva to Jaen cost?

6 Oh, no! These sneakers are d_____ , but they're the only ones in the store. I don't want to buy them.

4 Find somebody in your class who ...

1 has exchanged something for something else.

2 knows whose head is on a British pound coin.

3 has a receipt in their backpack.

4 prefers to read books than watch movies.

5 likes horseback riding.

6 likes grocery shopping.

5 Imagine you bought one of these items today. You regret buying it. Say:

how much it cost

why you bought it

why you regret buying it

what you did / you're going to do now

The T-shirt cost ...

4 Getting about

My goal

Mission Complete!

I can read and understand a text about a famous person.

5

I can answer questions on a story about time travel.

3

I can have a conversation about traveling and vacations.

4

I can talk about items using different tenses.

1

I can do a word puzzle.

2

And I need ...

To do this, I will ...

So I can ...

I want to practice ...

⊛ Diary

What I already know about traveling and transportation ...

What I have learned about traveling and transportation ...

1 Look and complete the sentences.

1 Do you think Toby's going to t a k e o f f ?

2 Amelia has her
b ___ r d ___ g
p ___ s ready.

3 Salvador has found a nice watch in the
d ___ t ___-f r ___ store at the airport.

4 The f ___ g h ___ to Munich is going to be late.

5 The airplane is going to l ___ d close to the beach.

6 The p ___ l ___ t s are flying the airplane.

2 Find the words and answer the questions.

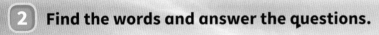

e c h k c n i

r t d p a u e r s e

t a e g

a c h e x e n g e t r a

i v a a r r s l

e n o u a n t n c e n m

1 What do you do before you go through security? _____ check in _____

2 Which part of the airport does a flight leave from? _____

3 What do you have to walk through to get to your airplane? _____

4 What tells you how many dollars you can buy for 100 euros? _____

5 Where in an airport can you meet friends coming from another country? _____

6 What should you listen for in an airport? _____

3 Complete the messages with words from Activities 1 or 2.

1 I spoke to the _____ at the door of the airplane. She's named Francesca, and her favorite airplane to fly is the Boeing 747.

2 The _____ at the airport isn't very good. Remember to change your money before you leave home.

1 🎧 5.10 **Listen to the interview.** (Circle) **the words that you <u>don't</u> hear.**

arrivals   boarding pass   departures   first aid   flight
jetlag   passenger   pilot   safety   take off

2 🎧 5.11 **Listen to the interview again and choose the correct answers.**

1   When Karl started to work as a flight attendant,

   A   he saw it as a good way to use his language skills.

   B   he thought he would do it for a limited period.

   C   he wanted to go to many different places.

2   What surprised some people about Karl's flight attendant training?

   A   how short it was

   B   where it took place

   C   what subjects it covered

3   At the start of a flight, Karl gets annoyed with passengers who

   A   have too much luggage.

   B   want to change seats.

   C   ask lots of questions.

4   What does Karl think he is particularly good at?

   A   communicating with people

   B   managing his time

   C   solving problems

5   Karl says people are wrong if they think that flight attendants

   A   have fun when they're working.

   B   see a lot of the world.

   C   earn good money.

6   Karl thinks he should spend more of his free time

   A   developing certain skills.

   B   meeting people.

   C   staying in shape.

3   **In pairs, say why you would/wouldn't like to be a flight attendant.**

I would love to be a flight attendant because I would be able to travel everywhere!

★ Grammar: review of passive forms

1 **Complete the sentences with the correct form of the verb in parentheses.**

1 "We are sorry to announce that all flights to Australia __have been canceled__ today." (cancel)

2 The final announcement _____ yet. Quick – let's run! (not make)

3 A boarding pass _____ to every passenger at check in. Don't lose it! (give)

4 Headphones _____ on the airplane. Remember to bring some if you want to watch a movie. (not provide)

5 We _____ at security because I had a plastic snake in my backpack. (stop)

6 This picture of my uncle flying an airplane _____ by my grandfather. (take)

2 **Complete the second sentences so that they mean the same as the first.** Use the passive.

1 We make this ice cream with eggs, sugar, cream, and broccoli.

   This ice cream ____is made____ with eggs, sugar, cream, and broccoli.

2 Sarah has opened Sally's present!

   Sally's present _____ Sarah!

3 I'm sorry, but we haven't found your backpack or coat.

   I'm sorry, but your backpack and coat _____ .

4 I lost my boarding pass somewhere between check in and the gate.

   My boarding pass _____ somewhere between check in and the gate.

5 We don't wear bathing suits to school.

   Bathing suits _____ to school.

6 I didn't tell Diego and Mateo about my birthday party.

   Diego and Mateo _____ about my birthday party.

3 **In pairs, choose one of the objects.** Make three passive sentences.

present (it is used …)   present perfect (it has been used …)   simple past (it was used …)

> This is a money box. It is used to contain coins. It was made in a factory. It has been broken into small pieces.

money box

boat

toys

washing machine

ice hockey stick

rain boots

1 **Look and complete the crossword.** Write a form of transportation using the yellow letters.

1

2

3

4

		1				
2						
		3				
4						

The form of transportation is ⁵ _____ .

2 **Read and complete the signs.**

Open your ¹ _passport_ to the page with the picture. Thank you!

Joe's ² _____ Hostel: ten-bed rooms available here. Lots of space for backpacks. Breakfast included!

Don't eat fast food in the ⁵ _____. There are specific eating areas in other parts of the station.

isaac travel reading

Never travel without information on the country you're visiting. To buy ⁶ _____ to all countries in Asia, please go to www.isaactravelreading.com.

Remember to be at the bus stop ten minutes early. Your ³ _____ , Helena, will be waiting to welcome you! Only two pieces of ⁴ _____ per person on the bus.

Attention all drivers of trucks and other tall vehicles! Please DON'T use the ⁷ _____ .

3 **Find five differences.** Write sentences.

A

B

_____

_____

_____

_____

Grammar: phrasal verbs and the object

1 **Write the words in the correct blank.** Cross out the blank you don't need.

> baking   his little sister   talking   ~~the dog~~   us   your seatbelt

1   It was raining, so I kept _____the dog_____ in the house _____✕_____ .
2   I was late because my neighbor kept _____ on _____ .
3   Our son, Richard, checked _____ in _____ before we went to the airport.
4   Put _____ on _____ . We're going to take off.
5   On weekends, James takes _____ care of _____ .
6   Next year, I'm going to take _____ up _____ .

2 **Order the words to make sentences.** There are two possible answers, but write one.

1   give / of / Please / end / back / the day. / gloves / my / by / the

_____

2   a / remember / very / can't / where! / important thing / I / put / but / away / I

_____

3   throw away / my / Don't / passport!

_____

4   TV / you / off / bed. / the / before / Turn / go to

_____

Speaking

3  **Watch Pablo and Ezgi do some speaking practice. Complete the sentences.**

1   _____ , I like traveling by airplane.
2   There are lots of things to see in my country, _____ , interesting towns …
3   … beautiful landscapes, seasides, _____ .
4   _____ , um, Italy, I think.

4 📝 **Now plan your answers to the questions.**

How do you like to travel when you go on vacation?

Where would you like to go on vacation next?

What do you like to take with you when you travel?

5 ▶ **Watch again and circle the stressed words.**

1   Well, I like traveling by airplane.
2   I think I would rather go to a different country.
3   I like to travel by boat or train. I'm scared of flying.

> **PRONUNCIATION TIP!**
> When expressing your preferences, stress the noun.

1 **How do you think the characters in the story feel?** Use sentences from the story to explain your answers.

1 How does the family feel when they arrive at the airport?

2 How does Billy feel when he sees the samurai and the ninjas?

3 How does the pilot feel when he tells the family he's run out of time-traveling gas?

4 How does Carla feel when the pilot explains that they're stuck in feudal Japan?

2 **What do you think happens in the next chapter of the story?** In pairs, discuss the following ideas and think of some more.

1 Billy finds out that the people in the town can actually see him.
2 Carla finds a way to make time-traveling gas, and the family fly on to the Triassic to see the dinosaurs.
3 The pilot finds a way to make time-traveling gas but flies away by himself, leaving the family in feudal Japan.
4 More time-travelers arrive in the town. They have extra time-traveling gas on their airplane.

FACT!

In 1895, the English writer H.G. Wells published the science-fiction novel *The Time Machine*. Wells was not the first to write about time travel, but he made going back and forth through time in a special vehicle a popular idea in stories. "Time machine" is the phrase Wells used to describe the vehicle in his story. Writers, scientists, and movie makers still use it today.

3 **Read and answer the questions.**

1 Would you rather travel into the future or the past?

2 If you could go back in time, which period of history would you go to and why?

Five sentences have been removed from the article. For each blank, choose the correct sentence. There are three extra sentences which you do not need to use.

Have you heard of CHRONOS AIRWAYS? I'm sure you have. After all, it's the only airline in the world that gives you the chance to travel back and forth in time! ¹ ☐ We went into the future, to the year 2101. I still can't believe we did it.

When my friend Elaine Farmar first told me about CHRONOS, I thought she was joking. I've read *The Time Machine* and seen the *Back to the Future* movies, but I've never thought that any of it was possible. Time travel is science fiction, isn't it? However, when Elaine showed me the family's round-time tickets and told me about their plans to go to Peru during the Age of the Incas, I realized she was telling the truth. ² ☐ I just couldn't get it out of my mind, so I booked tickets to travel into the future.

Traveling with CHRONOS is just like traveling with any other airline. You go to an airport, get on an airplane, sit in your seat, fasten your seatbelt, and wait to take off. Everything is normal. ³ ☐ Somehow you have traveled in time. When we landed in 2101, we realized right away that we were entering a new world. ⁴ ☐ However, when they spoke, they sounded just like you or me.

One of the most interesting things was the talking screens. They were in the walls, the trees, and the chairs. ⁵ ☐ You'll have to travel to the future and find out for yourself. However, let me tell you this – it's going to be very interesting!

A I don't want to say too much about the screens and what they do.

B But when you land, everything is different.

C Last spring, my family and I went on a trip with them.

D We didn't believe them.

E I think everyone wanted the same thing.

F From that moment on, it was the only thing I could think of.

G There weren't people at the airport, only robots.

H I decided not to say anything to them.

Read the sentences before and after each space very carefully. They will help you decide the right sentence to fill the space.

1 **Correct the sentences about Amy Johnson.**

1 Amy Johnson was an American pilot.

_____

2 She left London to fly to Australia on July 1, 1930.

_____

3 Amy had to fly during the night to try to break the record.

_____

4 She lost a lot of days because of engine problems.

_____

5 She took 15 days to fly from London to Australia.

_____

2 **Look at Amy's route on the map.** Circle the cities she flew over.

London – Vienna – Constantinople (Istanbul) – Sourabaya – Calcutta – Bangkok – Singapore – Port Darwin

3 **In pairs, match the countries to the cities.**

the U.K.   Thailand

India   Indonesia

Australia   Singapore

Turkey   Austria

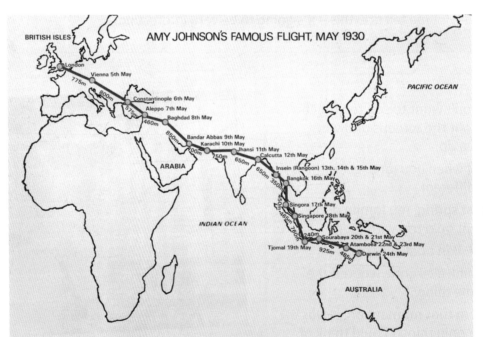

4 **Write different ways you can travel in the air.**

_____

_____

_____

_____

1 For each question, choose the correct answer.

The young people below all want to go abroad to a summer camp in Canada. Decide which summer camp would be the most suitable for each of them. For questions 1–5, match to the correct letter (A–H).

1 Yolanda wants a summer camp that offers challenging cycling trips with an expert who'll give her cycling tips. She also has plenty of experience with horses and wants to be able to go horseback riding.

2 Lucas is looking at a summer camp that's at least a month long. He wants to play team sports and see professional athletes competing.

3 Maya wants a camp that offers daily yoga sessions. She's an experienced diver who wants an instructor's advice to help her progress from intermediate to advanced dives.

4  Haruto enjoys getting involved in team activities while spending time in nature. He'd like to learn how to camp in challenging outdoor conditions and learn some historical facts about the local culture.

5 Katrin's an excellent surfer and wants a camp where she can surf and try out other extreme sports. She'd also like to take part in a project that's helping the environment.

Canadian Summer Camps

A Camp-Connect teaches teenagers how to stay safe, warm, and well fed while camping and hiking through an ancient forest in Western Canada. It's essential you like working in a group to achieve these extremely important skills. Camp leaders will also discuss the traditions of native Indians who come from this area.

B Tide's Up is a one-month surfing camp for the less experienced surfer. You'll start on gentle waves until you progress to the next level. You'll also develop team map-reading skills on some challenging forest hikes.

C Camp Tofino is a fun-filled, month-long camp. Wake up to catch waves at one of Canada's best surfing locations, followed by daily windsurfing and rock climbing lessons with local experts. An interest in protecting sea life is essential because you'll be taking care of rescued leatherback turtles that are in danger.

D The Wildteen Camp is a three-week camp for teens who are confident at either surfing, diving, or sailing. Our highly qualified water sports coaches will give you the support you need in order to improve to the next level in your chosen sport. Wake up to morning yoga, before riding some waves.

E Camp Horizon is perfect for teens who love doing outdoor activities. You'll have access to a large network of easy to advanced paths for hiking, and for horseback and bike riding. Go on daily rides with national champion Lorraine Ross, who'll give personal advice on how to improve your bike riding technique.

F Camp Canuck offers a wide range of individual and team sports. The facilities are suitable for learning basic horseback riding skills and for going on easy historical trail rides. Volleyball and hiking expeditions are just a few of the many activities on offer.

G Kool Kamp is for teenagers who want to improve their basketball and soccer skills. You'll follow a strict practice schedule, with coaches advising you, so you'll keep improving. It's not all hard work, though! You'll go to several professional games over this six-week camp.

H Coquihalla Camp is perfect for cyclists, at any level, who want qualified coaches to help them improve at cycling. Expect healthy eating and daily yoga sessions are part of the practice program at this six-week camp.

My progress: ____ /5

1 **Work in groups of three: one teacher and two students, A and B.**

 A and B: close your books and listen to the teacher.

 Teacher: read and use a timer.

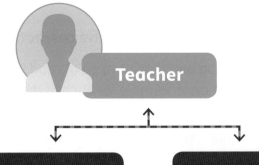
Teacher

Student A

Student B

 Now, I'd like each of you to talk by yourself about something. I'm going to give each of you a picture, and I'd like you to talk about it.

 A, here is your picture. It shows someone getting ready for a trip. B, you just listen.

Show Student A picture 1.

 A, please tell us what you can see in your picture.

Listen to A for one minute.

 Thank you.

B, here is your picture. It shows someone helping someone. A, you just listen.

Show Student B picture 2.

B, please tell us what you can see in your picture.

Listen to B for one minute.

 Thank you.

1

2

My progress:		
I understood and answered all the questions. ☐	I understood and answered most of the questions. ☐	I didn't understand all the questions and needed some help. ☐

1 **Write sentences using the words and the correct form of the verb.**

1   Delicious spicy curry / make / in this restaurant

Delicious spicy curry is made in this restaurant.

2   All flights / to Canada / cancel / today

_____

3   Tennis / not play / with a basketball

_____

4   The Eiffel Tower / complete / 1889

_____

5   The backpacker's passport / not find / yet

_____

6   We / not invite / to Michael's birthday party

_____

2 **Complete the sentences with the correct words in the box.**

> airplane   ~~back~~   down   find   for   ~~give~~   hamster   it   out   takes   them   up

1   It's my passport – ____give____ it ____back____ ! Please don't look at the picture!

2   I can't find my headphones anywhere. Can you help me look _____ , please?

3   Sit down, please. The _____ off in five minutes.

4   Put my _____ , please. She doesn't like being held. Oh, no! Did she bite you?

5   Look at the kitchen! Why is there flour on the floor? Clean _____ NOW!

6   I'm sorry. I don't know when the airplane to Timbuktu leaves. I'll _____ now.

3 **Read and write the correct word.**

1   This is a person who has studied for a long time and is now in charge of an airplane. ____pilot____

2   If you have a bad accident, this will take you to the hospital very quickly. _____

3   This is the part of the building where airplanes take off from. _____

4   This person carries all of his or her things in a large backpack and travels to different places. _____

5   This tells you how many pounds you can buy for your dollars. _____

6   This person knows a lot about a place and explains things to visitors. _____

4 **In pairs, answer the questions.**

What do you put in your hand luggage before you go on vacation?   ⤙ I always put my …

Think of a movie or book with an airport in it. What happens?   ⤙ I like the movie _Home Alone_. The family …

Would you like to be a pilot? Why / Why not?   ⤙ I wouldn't like to be a pilot because …

Review ••• Units 3–4

1 Complete the sentences with the correct form of the verbs in the box.

call pass read show speak ~~throw away~~ wear

1 I'll throw away your stuff if you leave it on the floor!
2 A boarding pass _____ at the door of a plane.
3 "_____ you _____ your grandma recently?" "Yes, I did. I _____ to her yesterday."
4 We _____ a bestseller in class this week.
5 I'm confident that he _____ the exam because he always works very hard.
6 It's definitely a bracelet. It _____ in Egypt.

2 👁 Find the mistake in each sentence. Re-write the sentences correctly.

1 He was show where to put his luggage. Then he said hi to everyone else.

   He was shown where to put his luggage. Then he said hi to everyone else.

2 I was working as a tour guide since July last year, and I love my job.

   _____

3 The pilot he is named Robert, and he works full time.

   _____

4 We are saw our local politician in the town this weekend.

   _____

5 I don't take a cab to the airport because my mom's going to drive me.

   _____

6 Next semester, I'm going to take after the violin. I wanted to learn how to play it.

   _____

3 Complete the sentences with the correct form of the verbs in the box.

be buy drink eat learn swim

1 _____ other languages is important if you want to travel.
2 Harriet would love _____ a pilot.
3 I'm not interested in _____ . I don't feel hungry.
4 _____ is great exercise.
5 My mother promised _____ new shoes for me.
6 I hate _____ coffee at night.

1 **Read Julie's text about shopping on vacation.**

Do you like shopping? I do. And I like taking vacations. I like to shop for special things when I am traveling. I sometimes buy something for myself. But I don't mind spending money on things my family likes. I usually shop for clothes or things that are from the place I visited on vacation. I always think about how much things cost, and I look for things that are on sale. I always use cash. When I come home, I have money from other countries because I can't spend it all.

2 **You are going to write about shopping on vacation. Make some notes.**

1 Things you buy on vacation: _____

2 Who you buy things for: _____

3 How much you like (or don't like) to shop: _____

4 Do you look for bargains? _____

5 How do you pay for the things you buy? _____

3 **Now do the task in Activity 2. Use your notes. Write your text in about 100 words.**

_____
_____
_____
_____
_____
_____
_____
_____
_____
_____

5 Study smarter

My goal

I can write an article about projects for a school website. **5**

Mission Complete!

I can read and understand a text about an environmental project. **3**

4 I can ask for clarification in a conversation.

1 I can read and understand advertisements or notes.

I can read a text and identify the missing sentences. **2**

And I need ...

To do this, I will ...

So I can ...

I want to practice ...

⊛ Diary

What I already know about study techniques ...

What I have learned about study techniques ...

1 Read and complete the crossword puzzle.

Down

1 A sheet of paper you can get when you pass an exam.

Across

2 If you're a beginner, you start at … 1.
3 This is a detailed piece of work with pictures. It's usually done in groups.
4 These are at the top of a test paper. They tell you what to do.
5 This is how well you do on a test.
6 This is a written piece of work about a specific topic.

Crossword:

Down 1: c e r t i f i c a t e
Across 2: e (_ _ _)
Across 3: (_ _ _ _ _ _)
Across 4: i (_ _ _ _ _ _ _ _ _ _)
Across 5: a (_ _ _)
Across 6: e (_ _ _ _)

2 Read and complete the texts.

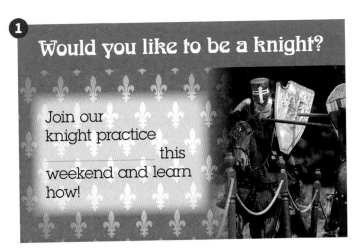

1

Would you like to be a knight?

Join our knight practice _____ this weekend and learn how!

2

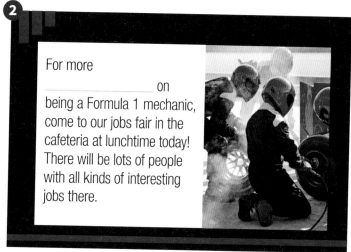

For more _____ on being a Formula 1 mechanic, come to our jobs fair in the cafeteria at lunchtime today! There will be lots of people with all kinds of interesting jobs there.

3

Choose your after-school activities for the summer _____ . There are a lot of things to enjoy before summer vacation. There's a choice of cricket, track and field, and water skiing on the lake. Not interested in sports? Take a look at the website for other indoor options, including filmmaking and a book club.

4

Remember your history _____ tomorrow. I expect a good grade, no excuses!
Love, Mom

Five sentences have been removed from the article. For each blank, choose the correct sentence. There are three extra sentences that you do not need to use.

The Memory Competition

It was a cold and gray morning when our teacher, Mr. Holmes, announced that our school would compete in the Junior Memory Championship. ¹_____ "Do you know, Clara, that I have a great memory?," said my friend Emily. "I know all the times tables up to 14 times 14."

"That's nothing," said Kyle. "I always get 10 out of 10 on my spelling tests, don't I, Clara?"

"I know you both have a good memory," I said. "Quiet now," said Mrs. Frank, our class teacher. "I'll assign you some challenges, and the two best students can go to the competition."

We spent the rest of the semester doing memory tests. I learned the names of trees, the dates of kings and queens, and lots and lots of phone numbers. ²_____
"I imagine numbers as pictures. So, for me, the number five is a hand, because we have four fingers and a thumb on each hand," explained Kyle.

"That sounds very complicated," I said. "I like to sing the numbers when I walk to school."

"I suppose we all learn in different ways. I use pictures. You use songs."

³_____ "Clara and Mario have the highest grades, so they're going to the competition. Good luck!"

The day of the competition arrived. There were children from many different schools there. We all went into a big room with our teachers and listened carefully to the instructions. Then we were ready for our first test. We had to remember 35 words, in the correct order.

⁴_____ "Tony the crocodile wears pajamas

when he plays board games in rockets to space with his vegetarian friends ... "

It was my turn. "Crocodile, pajamas, board games, rocket, space, vegetarian ... "

I got all 35 words right.

There were lots more tests I had to take. For example, I had to try and remember the names and faces of 40 people. I also had to remember a long list of numbers. ⁵_____ There were hundreds!

Unfortunately, I didn't win, but Mario and I both had a great time. When I saw Mr. Holmes, he said, "Good job, Clara! But you don't have an excuse for forgetting your homework now!"

A   Everyone found it very difficult.

B   I invented a silly song and sang it silently in my head.

C   Mario and I wrote an essay about the competition.

D   For each challenge, we had limited amounts of time to memorize everything.

E   We were all very excited when we heard this.

F   Emily and I talked about how we memorized these things.

G   I found drawing pictures for all the words was very helpful.

H   Then Mr. Holmes made the announcement we were all waiting for.

Grammar: simple past and present perfect time phrases

1 **Complete the sentences with the correct form of the verbs in parentheses.**

1 We _____ Legoland last month, and we went on all the rides. (visit)

2 I _____ just _____ the instructions, but I still can't make the robot. (read)

3 _____ you _____ your project on space yet? You have to hand it in today. (finish)

4 _____ you _____ a certificate for MVP yesterday? (get)

5 Pedro _____ to Juan Pablo since the start of semester, but I don't know why. (not speak)

2 **Match the sentence halves (1–5) to their endings (A–E).**

1 Junjie completed his homework

2 Danny joined the Manchester United youth team

3 Gael has never watched a game

4 Luciana has been upset about her grades

5 Gaspar hasn't commented on my pictures

A since the end of semester.

B at the Türk Telekom Stadium.

C yet. Maybe he will later.

D six weeks ago.

E 30 seconds before the teacher came into the room.

3 **Read, circle, and complete.**

1
Have you received a certificate for swimming?
(How did you feel? What did you do after?)

 Yes, when I was seven. Very happy! I ate cupcakes to celebrate!

2
Have you helped a stranger?
(Who was it? What did you do? How did you feel after?)

3
Have you made something to wear?
(What was it? What color was it? Who was it for? Were you happy with it?)

4
Have you watched a movie in English?
(What was the movie? Was it interesting? Was it easy to understand?)

5
Have you met a famous person?
(Who was it? Where did you meet them? What were they like?)

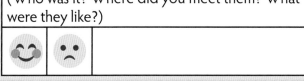

6
Have you visited a relative in a different city?
(Who was the relative? Where do they live? What did you do there?)

1 Order the letters and write the words.

idnfcntoe _____confident_____

lideedgth _____

tediesnert _____

drebo _____

suvoner _____

mlca _____

itedexc _____

deriwor _____

2 Use the words in Activity 1 to complete the sentences.

1 I wasn't _____bored_____ at the castle, I was just _____ about falling. The tour guide's talk was very interesting.

2 I was _____ in the presentation for the first hour, but after that, I fell asleep. Sorry!

3 I know you're scared of water, but there's no reason to be _____ . Just stay _____ , breathe deeply, and swim through the cave.

4 I was _____ when I heard that Eddie Redmayne was Newt Scamander in *Fantastic Beasts and Where to Find Them*. I'm _____ about the next movie!

5 I'm usually very _____ about tests, but I don't think I did very well on our end-of-year math test. Did I study enough?

3 🎧 5.12 Listen and number the pictures in order.

A

B

C

4 🎧 5.13 Listen again. Choose the best word and give reasons.

1 Mrs. Palmer is **nervous** / **calm**. _____

2 James is **bored** / **interested**. _____

3 Chloe is **excited** / **worried**. _____

★ Grammar: past perfect

1 **Complete the sentences with the past perfect of the verbs in the box.**

> be   just lock   ~~never win~~   not speak   not visit   tell

1   I'd never won ____ a competition before, but I have now!
2   He ____ the door when the phone rang.
3   They ____ the castle before, but they'd read about it.
4   It ____ a cold, dark day, and then the sun came out.
5   We ____ our aunt that we were scared of the dark, but she didn't believe us.
6   She ____ to the man with the tall black hat before today.

2 **Complete the text with the correct form of the verbs in parentheses.**

I ¹'d never been ____ (never be) to London before, but our class was doing a history project last semester, and so we planned a trip. Before we went, we ² ____ (choose) which places to go to. Our teacher ³ ____ (check) the prices and flight times, and we ⁴ ____ (make) a plan. I was so excited! Our first stop was the Tower of London. It was the place where prisoners were held if they ⁵ ____ (upset) the king or queen in the past. Sometimes, though, the prisoners ⁶ ____ (not do) anything wrong: Queen Elizabeth I was put in prison because her sister, Queen Mary, thought Elizabeth ⁷ ____ (want) to be queen instead. It was an amazing trip.

Speaking

3 **Watch Ezgi and Pablo do some speaking practice.** Number the expressions in order.

1   I'm sorry, could you say that again, please? ☐
2   Oh, sorry, I don't understand. ☐
3   Could you repeat the question, please? ☐

4 **Now plan your answers to the questions.**

How much homework do you do at home?

Do you know a good way to organize your time?

What was your last school project?

SPEAKING TIP! To hear a question again, remember to ask politely for help. Don't just say "What?"

5 ▶ **Watch again and write. What phrases can you use to ask for clarification?**

1   ____
2   ____
3   ____

PRONUNCIATION TIP! When asking for clarification, stress the word you don't understand.

1 Complete the graphic organizer about the story.

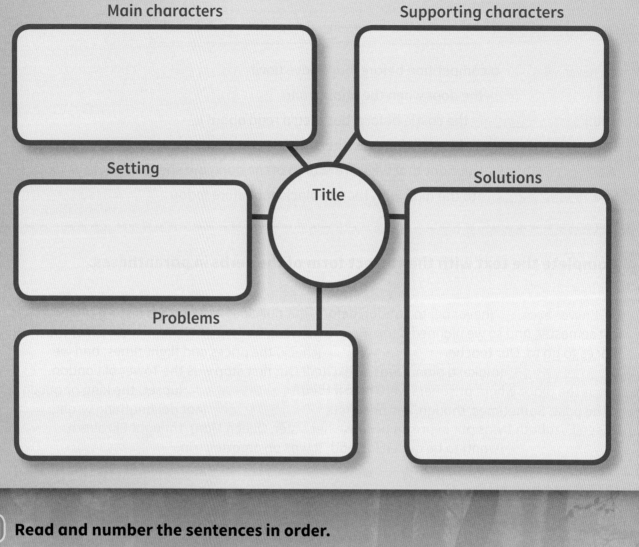

Main characters

Supporting characters

Setting

Title

Solutions

Problems

2 Read and number the sentences in order.

☐ They arrived very late at the campground.

1 Joe and Natalie arranged a camping trip.

☐ Next day, Sophie found the tent poles in the forest.

☐ They didn't find the tent poles, so they slept under the stars.

☐ Sophie didn't want to go camping.

☐ They all sat around the campfire and told scary stories.

3 How do you think the bag of tent poles got into the forest? Write an explanation.

_____

_____

_____

4 Imagine you are sitting around the campfire. Which scary story would you tell?

I would tell a story my uncle told me about a cyclist who disappeared …

5 🎧 5.14 ⭐ **Listen to six short conversations.** For each question, choose the correct answer.

1 Which place are they going to visit?

 **A** ☐

 **B** ☐

 **C** ☐

2 What's the weather going to be like today?

 A ☐

 B ☐

 **C** ☐

3 Who's the guide?

 A ☐

 B ☐

 C ☐

4 What is the girl's favorite food?

 **A** ☐

 **B** ☐

 **C** ☐

5 Where are the man's binoculars?

 **A** ☐

 B ☐

 **C** ☐

6 What would the boy like to be when he's older?

 A ☐

 **B** ☐

 C ☐

My progress: ☐ /6

1 **Read the text again.** Compare schools today to schools 100 years ago.

A hundred years ago, there were about 60 students in a class. In my school, there are 25.

2 **Ask a grown-up member of your family about their school.** Write their answers.

1 Where did you go to school when you were my age?

2 How many children were in your class?

3 Were there boys and girls in your class?

4 What were your favorite subjects?

5 Did you use any kind of technology in the class?

6 What didn't you like about your school? Why?

3 **Write what you think schools will be like in 2117.**

I think schools will ...

1 For each blank, choose the correct word.

The cleaner harbors project

Clean Harbors is a water project that started in 2014. The owner, Yannis Metaxis, was anxious about the [1]... of pollution that he saw in the harbors when he went sailing. He felt extremely disappointed when he realized that some plant families had already disappeared. He opened a learning center next to the harbor, and now he [2]... children and adults about the connection between water and the natural world.

Field trips to this popular [3]... are mostly organized during the semester. As well as local plants, you can discover the life cycles and habitats of the [4]... marine life from the area.

Short courses are available for all ages and cover subjects such as recycling water and responsible tourism. Each course has a final test and, in [5]..., you receive a certificate to show what you have learned. Yannis and his team are [6]... that the next generation will take more care of the environment.

1	A	amount	B	height	C	length	D	size
2	A	learns	B	studies	C	informs	D	involves
3	A	scenery	B	monument	C	entertainment	D	attraction
4	A	depressed	B	different	C	disappointing	D	difficult
5	A	case	B	reserve	C	addition	D	request
6	A	confident	B	helpful	C	reliable	D	calm

My progress: ___/6

1 **Choose <u>one</u> of these questions.** Write your answer in about 100 words.

Question 1

You see this sign on a school's website.

Articles wanted!

<u>School Projects</u>

What is the best subject for a school project?

Is it the environment, the local town, or the weather? Do you prefer to work on school projects alone, or with a partner, or in groups? Why? Give us your opinions.

Write an article answering these questions, and we will publish the best ones on our website.

Write your article.

Question 2

- Write Your English teacher has asked you to write a story.
- Your story must begin with this sentence.

I read the instructions and felt confident. I decided to accept the challenge.

- Write your story.

_____

_____

_____

_____

_____

_____

_____

_____

_____

My progress: /5

1 **Complete the sentences with the simple past or present perfect form of the verbs in parentheses.**

1 I've been _____ to Florida lots of times, and I'm going again next year! (be)

2 We _____ calm when we went into the cave. We don't like dark spaces. (not be)

3 _____ a comment on my picture late last night? (post)

4 Carmen and Samuel _____ the cake yet, but they made it yesterday. (not decorate)

5 Anna _____ her leg skateboarding last weekend. (break)

6 She _____ field hockey for the school team since she was in middle school. (play)

7 He _____ delighted about winning the math competition. (look)

8 _____ the instructions correctly? We're on Step 4 now, but it doesn't look like a plane! (follow)

2 **Order the words to make sentences.**

1 because / disappointed / I was / really hard! / with my test grade / I'd tried

_____

2 before / her. / the email / She / Tim called / hadn't read

_____

3 his test, / five more questions. / he turned the page / He'd finished / found / and then / and

_____

4 the tickets / the car / They / when / were / they realized / 'd gotten into / on the kitchen table.

_____

3 **Complete the sentences with the correct words.**

1 I'm not sure what to do next. An art c o u r s e , or drama?

2 I know you're _____, but you could pretend to be interested in my class!

3 Yes, it's the last day of school. I know you're _____ . I am, too!

4 An _____ always has an introduction and a conclusion.

5 Don't worry. Stay _____, and you'll be fine!

6 The last day of the summer _____ is June 30 this year.

4 **Read the example.** Then, in pairs, discuss the other pictures.

> The boy with the number 27 on his shirt has won a competition and is delighted. The other boy was confident and thought he had won.

6 Good job!

Mission Complete!

I can write an email stating preferences and making suggestions. **5**

I can take part in a conversation and use common expressions. **3**

I can order pictures to indicate a process. **4**

I can read and understand people's opinions on jobs and work. **2**

I can read and understand information on business cards. **1**

My goal

And I need ...

To do this, I will ...

So I can ...

I want to practice ...

⊛ Diary

What I already know about jobs and work ...

What I have learned about jobs and work ...

1 Look and answer the questions.

| a cleaner | a hairdresser | a librarian | a musician | a politician | a sailor | a scientist | ~~an architect~~ |

1 Your parents have just bought this! Who should they call first?
   an architect

2 Lucia needs a haircut. Who should she see?
   _____

3 Oops! Somebody dropped a drink in the office kitchen. Who can help?

4 Who works here?
   _____

5 Who is going to come on stage?
   _____

6 What do you have to be to work here?
   _____

7 Who might tell them to be quiet?
   _____

8 Who speaks here?
   _____

2 Read and write the jobs.

1 Letters and packages delivered every day, in all weather, with a smile.
   mail carrier

2 I turn your great ideas into the next bestseller. Call me! June

3 I design great video games. Check out my website to see what I can do!

4 Enormous houses | Tiny apartments Modern hospitals
No project too big or too small. Call me to discuss.

5 amy@amycutsforyou.com Long, short, curly, or straight.
The perfect style, just for you!

6 Dirty floors? Mess everywhere? Great!
Matthew – making all surfaces shine

3 In pairs, say which three jobs you wouldn't like to do and why.

> I wouldn't like to be a scientist because …

1 🎧 5.15   **Listen and check (✓) the correct sentences.**

1   The two women have met before. ☐

2   The man talks about three different books. ☐

3   The man and woman get along well. ☐

4   The woman is the Prime Minister. ☐

5   One of the men is 22. ☐

6   A musical instrument breaks. ☐

2 🎧 5.16 ⭐   **Listen again. For each question, choose the correct answer.**

1   What will Sarah's hair look like when she leaves the hairdresser's?

A ☐   B ☐   C ☐

2   Which is the best cover for Tom's book?

A ☐   B ☐   C ☐

3   What's the woman's job?

A ☐   B ☐   C ☐

4   What's happening now?

A ☐   B ☐   C ☐

5   What job do the two speakers have?

A ☐   B ☐   C ☐

⭐ Grammar: modals of probability/deduction

1 Choose the correct words to complete the sentences.

1 Tom **can't** / **might** be a librarian – he doesn't like reading!

2 Camila **must** / **might** be a musician. She can play the guitar well, and I think she can sing.

3 It **could** / **must** be used for writing, but I'm not sure.

4 He **must** / **could** be a sailor. Only sailors are allowed on the boat.

5 Their new pet **can't** / **may** be a rat, or it might be a cat. I didn't hear what they said.

2 Match the sentences (1–6) to pictures (A–F). Then complete the sentences.

A 3   **B**  ☐   **C** ☐   **D** ☐   **E** ☐   **F** ☐

1 It _____ be angry, or it could be scared.

2 It _____ be a box, or it _____ be a glass cube. I'm very confused!

3 She _must_ be American. She has an American passport.

4 She _____ be on the tennis team today. She has a broken leg!

5 It _____ be midnight. Happy New Year!

6 He _____ be at the hairdresser's. He doesn't have much hair!

3 Read the notes and complete the sentences with *may, might, could, must,* or *can't.*

Ben gets to school at 8:20.
The first bus leaves at 7:45.
The trip takes 35 minutes.
The first train leaves at 8:30.

Emilia hates cheese, but she loves potatoes. She can't eat tomatoes, but she doesn't mind onions, fish, or pasta.

How does Ben get to school?

Ben ¹ _may_ take the bus to school, or he ² _____ walk. He ³ _____ travel by train.

What is Emilia going to order?

She ⁴ _____ order tortilla, or she ⁵ _____ choose tuna with pasta. She ⁶ _____ order pizza because it has tomatoes and cheese.

4 Write sentences with *may, might, could, must,* or *can't.*

The next president of the United States can't be Spanish.

_____

_____

_____

_____

_____

_____

_____

_____

1 **Look at the code and write the words.**

♥ a ▲ e ◆ i ■ o ⬡ u

1 __ ■ __ _____ boss _____   7 __ ▲ __ ◆ __ ▲ __ _____

2 ■ – __ ■ __ ▲ __ _____   8 ⬡ __ ▲ __ ■ ▲ __ _____

3 __ ◆ __ _____   9 __ ♥ __ ▲ ▲ __ _____

4 ♥ __ – __ ◆ __ ▲ _____   10 ▲ ♥ __ _____

5 ♥ __ ♥ __ _____   11 __ ⬡ __ – t ◆ __ ▲ _____

6 __ ♥ __ _____

2 **Complete the texts with the correct form of the words in Activity 1.**

If you want a ¹ _career_ as a musician, you need to start when you're young. This is Alma Deutscher. She plays the piano and violin and writes and performs her own operas!

Hi Jenny,
Guess what? I've decided to ² _____ my job! I don't really like my ³ _____ because she's always rude to me. Anyway, I've decided to leave to join the circus, or climb Mount Everest, or something! 😀
Speak soon,
Adrian

Next year I want to get a ⁴ _____ job, just during weekends and school vacations. I don't mind what I do, but if my ⁵ _____ are nice people, I'll be happy!

Kim,
Remember it's your dad's last day at work today before he ⁶ _____ . So, we're going out for dinner to celebrate. Don't forget!
Mom

Dear Aunt Fix-it,
I'm a bit worried about my sister, Sofia. She's 21 and she's ⁷ _____ right now. She can't afford to go out much because she doesn't ⁸ _____ any money. She's applied for jobs but had no luck. She's very smart, she's great with people, and she got excellent grades at college. What should she do next? Please help. Sam

I didn't spend much time with my parents when I was little because they set up their own travel business. Things improved after a few years, and they employed some ⁹ _____ . When I left school, I joined them, too. I work ¹⁰ _____ , and they pay me a good ¹¹ _____ . I work six days a week and enjoy every minute!

★ Grammar: present perfect progressive

1 **Complete the sentences with the correct form of the verbs in parentheses.**

1 I've been studying programming at college for three months. (study)
2 _____ David _____ you in your new job? I asked him to this morning. (help)
3 She _____ at her desk today. I don't know where she is. (not sit)
4 Trisha _____ as an architect for two years. She loves her job. (work)
5 Your co-workers _____ about you! They never talk about anyone. (not talk)
6 _____ you _____ for me for a long time? I'm so sorry I'm late. (wait)

2 **In pairs, order the words to make sentences.**

1 today / watching / Has / he / been / TV ?
2 been / a / reading / about / We've / great / Miley Cyrus. / article
3 been / you / Australia / How / traveling / have / long / around ?
4 been / their / doing / They / haven't / homework.

Speaking

3 **Watch Ezgi do some speaking practice. Listen and number.**

A OK. [1]
B What else can I say? [ ]
C ... or something like that. [ ]
D I mean ... [ ]
E What's the word? [ ]
F I guess. [ ]

4 **Watch again and say *yes* or *no*.**

1 Ezgi starts by saying what job the man does.
2 She knows what the diagram is.
3 She mentions some equipment in the room.
4 She says what he looks like.

5 **Imagine you're Pablo.** Look at the picture. **Describe it. Then listen to Pablo.**

> **SPEAKING TIP!** You can use small words/phrases like *OK* and *I mean* to give yourself more time to think. Just don't overuse them.

6 **Watch again and complete the sentences. Then** (circle) **the words that are stressed.**

1 I _____ he _____ be an architect because it looks like a plan of a building on the whiteboard.
2 It _____ be the plan of an office, or a hotel, or _____ like that.
3 I think the other people in the room _____ be his co-workers.
4 It _____ like a good meeting.

1 Answer the questions.

1 Why was Mike alone in the house so often?
Both his parents worked.

2 What was he working on in school?

3 Why does his project make him think about working now?

4 Was his father serious when he told Mike to start walking dogs?

5 How did Mike advertise his company?

6 Why has Mike stopped daydreaming?

2 Imagine you were opening a dog-walking company. Write the information you would put on the Internet.

The name of the company

Your contact information

The time of day for walks, and how long the walks are

What you charge

3 Design a card for your company using your notes from Activity 2.

Read this email from your English-speaking friend, Mike, and the notes you have made.

To:	Subject: Smart Dog Walking
From: Mike	

Hi, everyone. I've started a company to walk dogs after school every afternoon. I now have so many dogs to walk that I need help. Would you like to work with me? —————————— → Say yes

You can walk dogs one at a time or several together.

Tell Mike how many

I'm planning to offer extra dog services for the clients' dogs. What sorts of things do you think I could offer?

Suggest something

Of course, we get paid for every dog we walk, so you'd earn some money. ————————————— → Explain how much you want to earn

I hope you're interested in helping me.

Mike

Write your email to Mike in about 100 words, using the notes you have made.

To: Mike	Subject: Smart Dog Walking
From:	

1 **Look at the pictures and write the correct words from the box to identify the economic sector they belong to.**

construction   education   farming   food industry   ~~health~~   mining industry

health   _____   _____

2 **Read and answer *yes* or *no*.**

1   Primary sector workers produce natural products, or extract them from the ground.   _____
2   Teachers and bus drivers work in the secondary sector.   _____
3   Tertiary workers provide a service to customers.   _____
4   The secondary sector uses materials from the primary sector.   _____
5   The energy industry is part of the primary sector.   _____

3 **Find out what we can make from these raw materials.**

wheat   _____   cotton   _____
olives   _____   leather   _____
milk   _____   sand   _____
strawberries   _____   wood   _____

4 **Order the pictures.** Write a sentence about each step of the chain of production.

A
B  1
C

D
E
F

1 🎧 5.17 **For each question, choose the correct answer.**

You will hear an interview with a young musician named Danny.

1 When he was in school, Danny particularly enjoyed

    A playing music with his friends.

    B having individual lessons.

    C taking part in concerts.

2 Performing at parties helped Danny to

    A earn some extra money.

    B improve his songwriting skills.

    C feel more confident about playing in public.

3 How does Danny now feel about his first online music video?

    A impressed by the way he sang in it

    B surprised by how quickly it became popular

    C embarrassed by the number of mistakes in it

4 In making his latest album, Danny found it hard to decide

    A what order the songs should be in.

    B what style the music should be.

    C what picture should go with it.

5 What did Danny think of the festival he attended recently?

    A It had an interesting variety of bands.

    B It offered great value for money.

    C It was in a suitable location.

6 What does Danny plan to do next?

    A develop a new skill

    B move to a different country

    C work more with other musicians

My progress: ⬚/6

1 **For each blank, write the correct word.** Write <u>one</u> word for each blank.

Write your answers in **CAPITAL LETTERS** below the text.

Being a mail carrier

This job is pretty hard, even though it looks easy. I've learned a lot about neighborhoods and pets [1]… the years! Cats are usually friendly, but some dogs can be dangerous. The strangest animal I've seen at one [2]… the houses is a monkey in the front yard!

The first thing I do each day is sort the mail with my co-workers. After a short break, we each take our bag and start our route. I love being a mail carrier because I get to be connected with [3]… public. I deliver on foot, by bike, or with a small van. I have [4]… be prepared for all kinds of weather. For example, [5]… it's very rainy, I need to be careful not to get the flu.

Modern changes have been improvements to the uniform and encouraging more female workers. I feel more comfortable in the new uniforms, especially the summer one. Part-time or full-time training starts [6]… young as 16. I didn't start when I was 16, but I was only a couple of years older. This can lead to some interesting career opportunities in IT and business.

1 ☐☐☐☐☐

3 ☐☐☐☐☐

5 ☐☐☐☐☐

2 ☐☐☐☐☐

4 ☐☐☐☐☐

6 ☐☐☐☐☐

My progress: ☐ /6

6

1 Complete the text with *may*, *might*, *could*, *must*, or *can't*. Use each verb only once. There is more than one possibility.

In this picture, there's a man in a blue suit and a red tie who is talking. There are people listening to him. I think they ¹_____ be his co-workers. There's a red, white, and blue flag behind him, so I think they ²_____ be in the U.S.A. He ³_____ be a musician because he doesn't have an instrument, and he isn't singing. I don't know his name, but he ⁴_____ be a politician because he looks important. He ⁵_____ want to be the next President of the United States.

2 Complete the sentences with the correct form of the verbs in the box.

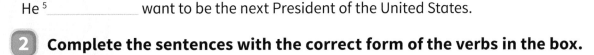

cook   drive   paint   play   sunbathe   ~~take care of~~

1 I'm really tired because I've been taking care of our new puppy all day.

2 We _____ on the beach all day. We've been swimming in the sea.

3 Vincente _____ in the kitchen. He's been making a vlog.

4 _____ Sofia _____ her bedroom this morning?

5 Toby _____ video games all day.

6 Which car _____ today?

3 Read and complete the crossword puzzle.

Down

1 When somebody doesn't have a job, they are …

5 Someone you work with is a …

Across

2 Someone who designs buildings is an …

3 Someone who decides which books are written is a …

4 When you stop working permanently, usually when you're in your 60s, you …

6 Someone who sometimes works in a laboratory is a …

Crossword down 1: u n e m p l o y e d

4 What does the man in the picture do? Where does he work? Who does he work with?

I think he must be a …

Review ● ● ● Units 5–6

1 **Complete the definitions.**

1 A _certificate_ is something you receive when you've done well in a competition or passed an exam.

2 A _____ is someone whose job involves playing an instrument or singing.

3 A person is _____ when they feel unhappy because something is not interesting.

4 A person is _____ when they feel peaceful.

5 A _____ is someone who works on a ship.

6 A _____ is the person who is in charge at work.

2 **Choose the correct answers to complete the sentences.**

1 Beth **didn't win** / (**hadn't won**) a prize before today.

2 Before last year, my sister **hadn't been** / **wasn't** a hairdresser.

3 After he saw his grade, David **was** / **had been** happy.

4 Daniel and Sara **had been working** / **worked** for the same company for two years before they met.

5 Jane **went** / **had gone** to the movies last night.

3 **Complete the sentences with the correct word from the box.**

> a librarian   an essay   a politician   confident   nervous

1 In school, we sometimes have to write _____ .

2 I am really _____ when I swim because I'm afraid of sharks.

3 When I want to find a book, I ask _____ for help.

4 The president is _____ who works for the country.

5 Lucy felt _____ that she would do well on the test.

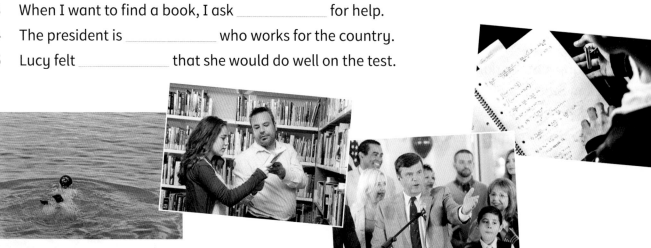

1 **Read this email from your English-speaking friend, Jo.**

To:	
From:	Jo

Yes – say what

Hi,

I'm so glad you're allowed to visit me this summer. You must be very excited! ———————————————— Yes!

I know it's your first time flying by yourself, so try not to worry. Since it's a long flight, what are you going to take with you so you aren't bored?

I have to do a school project during the vacation. Will you have any homework?

Tell Jo what

Mom and I will pick you up from the airport. What would you like to do during your visit?

Don't forget your passport!

See you soon,   Suggest something

Jo

2 **Read Jo's email. Make notes about how you will answer her questions.**

1   Are you excited to visit Jo?

2   What will you do during the flight so that you aren't bored?

3   Will you have any homework?

4   What would you like to do when you visit Jo?

3 **Now write an answer to Jo's email using your notes. Write your answer in about 100 words.**

In this activity, you need to include each response in your answer.

To:	Jo
From:	

7 It's the law!

My goal

I can listen to conversations and identify the main idea. **5**

Mission Complete!

I can understand a conversation with a partner and ask for their opinion. **3**

4 I can read and understand about fingerprints.

I can understand job definitions. **1**

I can read a text and answer questions on different laws. **2**

And I need …

To do this, I will …

So I can …

I want to practice …

Diary

What I already know about the law …

_____

_____

What I have learned about the law …

_____

_____

1 Read and label the items. Use the words in the box.

> article   cameraman   crime   criminal   ~~headline~~   interview   reporter

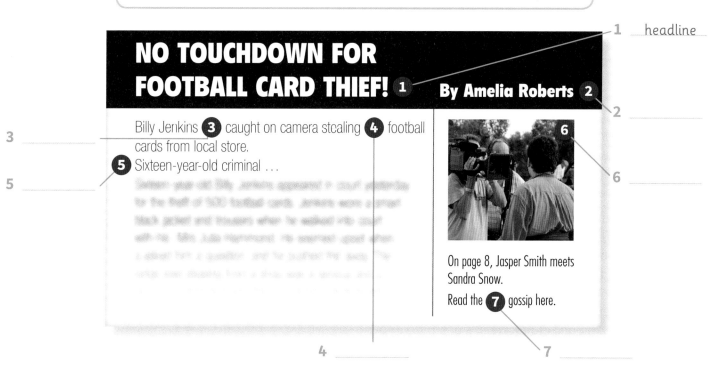

NO TOUCHDOWN FOR FOOTBALL CARD THIEF! 1   **By Amelia Roberts** 2

Billy Jenkins 3 caught on camera stealing 4 football cards from local store.

5 Sixteen-year-old criminal . . .

On page 8, Jasper Smith meets Sandra Snow.
Read the 7 gossip here.

1 ____headline____
2 _____
3 _____
4 _____
5 _____
6 _____
7 _____

2 Read and complete the definitions.

1 A judge is someone who says what punishment a criminal receives.

2 A _____ is someone who goes to court with someone who has problems with the law and advises them.

3 A _____ is someone who investigates crimes.

4 A _____ is someone who breaks the law.

5 A _____ is someone who writes about the crime in an article.

6 A _____ is someone who films the criminal walking into court.

3 Complete the article.

Sixteen-year-old ¹ __criminal__ Billy Jenkins appeared in court yesterday, under arrest for the theft of 500 football cards. Jenkins wore a black jacket and pants when he walked into court with his ² _____ , Mrs. Julia Hammond. He seemed upset when a ³ _____ asked him a question, and he pushed the ⁴ _____ away. The judge said stealing from a store was a serious ⁵ _____ , and a serious punishment was the only option. Jenkins will spend 100 hours picking up trash from outside the local stores and parks. ⁶ _____ Ashton, who investigated the crime, said she was happy with the result.

For each question, choose the correct answer.

Police officer Simon Holmes talks about his job

I decided to become a police officer because I like the idea of helping people and making the world a safer and better place. Before I could go out in my uniform, I had to learn lots of laws that exist here in England. The majority of them are obvious – we all know that we aren't allowed to steal things, or drive too fast, or go through red traffic lights. But then I found some really unusual ones!

Imagine you're invited to a costume party while you're on vacation here in the U.K. There are lots of people you could dress up as, but if you're caught wearing a sailor's uniform, you could go to jail for three months. So, you should bring something else to wear instead. While you're packing your luggage, it's useful to know that you can bring potatoes from anywhere in the world, just not Poland. You probably won't get through security at the airport if you have a few Polish potatoes in your backpack. If you follow our laws, you won't get arrested and you'll have a great time and leave with happy memories. Don't even think about putting a stamp on a postcard upside down. It's against the law in the U.K.!

You might think our laws in England are a little odd, but I spoke to a detective from Italy. In his country, you aren't allowed to build sandcastles on a particular beach, or wear thongs if they're noisy. And if you see this headline, "Worker falls asleep in cheese factory," please don't laugh. It's a serious crime in Italy.

Of course, most of these strange laws are funny, and you probably wouldn't go to jail if you broke them, but it's a good reminder that before we travel anywhere new, we should always read about how to behave, so we don't get in trouble or upset people.

1   What does Simon say about most laws in the U.K.?

   A   There aren't many laws because it's a safe place.

   B   Most laws are about driving and traffic.

   C   Most laws are things that everybody knows.

   D   Only police officers understand them.

2   In the second paragraph, what is illegal in the U.K.?

   A   carrying potatoes from any countries in your backpack

   B   wearing a police officer's uniform

   C   tearing a postcard

   D   putting a stamp on something the wrong way

3   What mustn't you do in Italy?

   A   wear noisy footwear

   B   play sports on certain beaches

   C   laugh at newspapers

   D   visit cheese factories

4   What would be a good introduction to this article?

   A   Police officer Simon Holmes tells us about some surprising rules around the world.

   B   In this article, police officer Simon Holmes talks about his experiences of being a police officer in different countries.

   C   After being a policeman in the U.K. for many years, Simon Holmes retires and investigates strange laws in other countries.

   D   For police officer Simon Holmes, being a police officer is very boring. Here he tells us about his first year in the job.

Grammar: reported speech

1 **Look at the words in red. Choose the correct answers.**

1 "You're a criminal!" The judge said that I (was) / **had been** a criminal.

2 "Chloe didn't go to school today." Sarah said that Chloe **didn't go** / **hadn't gone** to school **that** / **this** day.

3 "Javier has broken a window." Mom said that Javier **breaks** / **had broken** a window.

4 "I can play volleyball on this beach." Xiang said that he **is able to** / **could** play volleyball on **that** / **this** beach.

5 "We'll go to Brazil next year." Matteo and Diego said that they **would go** / **are going** to Brazil **that** / **the following** year.

6 "Mia and I have to talk to Detective Fraser now." Mia said that she and Emma **must** / **had to** speak to Detective Fraser **then** / **now**.

2 🎧 5.18 **Re-write the sentences in reported speech.** Then listen and check your answers.

1 "I'm coming to your party tomorrow!" (Helen)

Helen said she was coming to my party the following day.

2 "I can't hang out with you today." (Renata)

_____

3 "You're talking to my sister." (Ben)

_____

4 "Aunt Sarah and Uncle James have arrived at our house." (Mom)

_____

3 **Read the messages from Sebi.** Complete the report in reported speech, with 1–3 words in each blank.

10:20	I'm in the café with Mandy. We're sitting next to the window.
10:21	There are lots of people we know here. They are all buying food
10:27	We have a great view of the street.
10:44	We can see two men on motorcycles.
10:45	There's a lot of noise. What should I do?
10:47	I'll call the police.

Earlier this morning, Sebi said he [1] __was__ in the café with Mandy. [2] _____ at a table next to the window. [3] _____ lots of people [4] _____ . Apparently, they all [5] _____ something to eat or drink. At just before half past ten, Sebi said that they [6] _____ a good view of the street. Then, at 10:44, Sebi sent another message. He said that he and Mandy [7] _____ two men on motorcycles. Just a minute later, there [8] _____ a lot of noise, and he asked what he [9] _____ do. Two minutes later, he said he [10] _____ call the police. I wonder what happened next?

interruptscreamwhispercomplainjokedemand

1 **Find six verbs in the wordsnake.**

2 **Complete the sentences with the correct verbs in Activity 1.**

1 One girl is w h i s p e r i n g to her friend in class. Our teacher said that was very rude.

2 That ride looks very scary. Did you _ _ _ _ _ _ when you were upside down?

3 The soccer player _ _ _ _ _ _ _ _ _ _ to the referees about their decision. He thought it was unfair.

4 Sally's mother _ _ _ _ _ _ _ about not having enough flour, when there was flour everywhere!

5 Rafael _ _ _ _ _ _ _ _ _ _ his father when he was working.

6 There are a lot of people in the streets. They're tired of things and are _ _ _ _ _ _ _ _ change.

3 🎧 5.19 **Listen and complete the sentences with the correct form of the verbs in the box.**

~~ask~~ claim complain demand interrupt joke ~~reply~~ scream suggest whisper

1 David _asked_ Mia what she thought of the headline. Mia _replied_ that it was shocking.

2 Fiona _____ going to the movies.

3 The librarian _____, "Be quiet!"

4 Jessica _____ about her vacation.

5 Gabriel _____ that he had been best friends with George Ezra since school.

6 Jimena _____ that he had looked like a clown.

7 Juan Diego _____ another pizza immediately.

8 Emily _____ that there was a snake in her room.

9 Beth _____ the tour guide to ask about breakfast.

4 **In pairs, say and guess the verb.**

Emma … that my dog had taken her sandwich.

Joked?

No, she wasn't laughing.

Screamed?

No, she wanted me to make her a new sandwich.

Oh, complained!

★ Grammar: Questions in reported speech

1 Complete with the correct form of *ask* and the missing words.

1 "When is your birthday?" She _asked when her_ birthday ___was___.
2 "Are you American?" He _____ I _____ American.
3 "Will you visit the Great Wall in China?" They _____ I _____ the Great Wall in China.
4 "Can you bake cupcakes, Clara?" Maria _____ Clara _____ bake cupcakes.
5 "Has your sister done her homework?" Mom _____ sister _____ her homework.
6 "Do you play tennis?" He _____ I _____ tennis.

2 Correct the mistakes in the sentences.

1 Lucia asked me if I can help her with her project. _____
2 Yan asked Jing how old was she. _____
3 Tomás asked Francesca she was going on the field trip. _____
4 Beatrice asked Lucas if he did had a laptop. _____
5 Felipe asked Bruno when leaves the bus. _____

Speaking

4 In pairs, discuss the situation below.

A school has won $1,000 to spend on anything they want.

> **SPEAKING TIP!** In a conversation, we usually ask each other questions to get more information and to keep the conversation going.

5 **Watch again and <u>underline</u> where the stress falls.** Mark the direction of the intonation.

That would be OK, wouldn't it?
I don't think that would be a fun job.

3 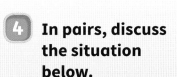 **Watch Ezgi and Pablo do some speaking practice. Check (✓) the questions you hear.**

A What do you think of …? ☐
B Why do you think that? ☐
C That would be OK, wouldn't it? ☐

> **PRONUNCIATION TIP!** Your feelings can affect how you express your opinion. When offering an opinion, think carefully about how strongly you want to express it.

1 Answer the questions about the story.

1 What did Robert McGinty do?

_____

2 What is Elizabeth Sanchez's job?

_____

3 Why was it hard to catch Robert McGinty?

_____

4 Did Elizabeth Sanchez catch Robert McGinty by herself?

_____

2 Read the sentences. Do you agree with them? Why / Why not? Discuss your ideas in a group.

1 Criminals like Robert McGinty should go to jail for a long time.

2 Criminals like Robert McGinty shouldn't go to jail. They should do work in the community to help other people.

3 Police officers should only try to catch criminals. It isn't their job to think about why people commit crimes.

4 We should help criminals change their behavior.

3 How can we stay safe online? Write your ideas below.

_____

_____

_____

4 In pairs, discuss your ideas from Activity 3.

FACT!

The world's first modern police force was London's Metropolitan Police Service. Set up in 1829 by a politician named Sir Robert Peel, the professional police officers who worked for the service became known as "bobbies" (Bobby is short for Robert). Some people in the U.K. still call police officers bobbies.

5 Find out about the police force in your country. Write four facts.

_____

_____

_____

6 **For each blank, choose the correct word.** Write <u>one</u> word in each space.

Write your answers in **CAPITAL LETTERS** below the text.

The day my identity was stolen

I'd just come home and turned my computer on. I was surprised to see a picture on the screen. It was of ¹… foot above a banana skin. Under the image there was a message. "Watch you don't slip!" ²… said.

When I realized that I couldn't delete the picture, I felt angry. I turned my computer off ³… on, but the picture was still there. I couldn't use my computer.

⁴… next day the bank told me there wasn't ⁵… money left in my account. I called the police. "You're not the only one," they said. "Somebody's been stealing people's identities online." I felt like such a fool. It took six months ⁶… get my money back.

1
☐☐☐☐☐

2
☐☐☐☐☐

3
☐☐☐☐☐

4
☐☐☐☐☐

5
☐☐☐☐☐

6
☐☐☐☐☐

Think of the part of speech that needs to fill each blank. For example, does the blank need a pronoun (it, she), an article (the, a), or a preposition (of, in)?

1 **Read and answer the questions**

1 When do the lines on our fingers and thumbs form?

_____

2 Explain how a fingerprint can identify a person.

_____

3 When did the police first use a fingerprint to solve a crime?

_____

4 Explain how technology can make police work easier.

_____

5 What should you do if you do not want to leave fingerprints?

_____

2 **Describe the fingerprints.** Find the two that are the same.

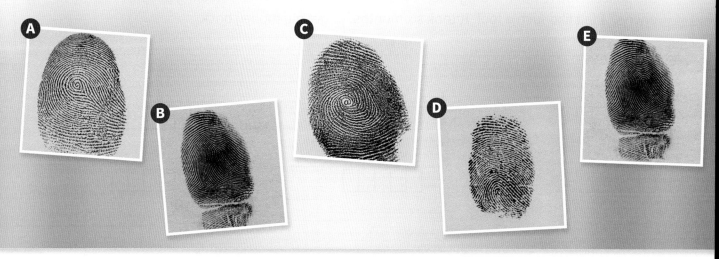

3 **Make a fingerprint.** In pairs, compare yours to your partner's.

Remember the words:

arches   My fingerprints

loops   _____

whorls   My partner's fingerprints
            _____

My fingerprints have …

4 **In pairs, read and answer the questions.**

1 What other ways can fingerprints be used for identification?

2 When will a fingerprint not help the police in their investigation?

3 Can you think of a material that will be difficult to find fingerprints on?

4 Why mustn't you touch anything at a crime scene?

Fingerprints can be used on identity cards and …

1 **For each question, choose the correct answer.**

Writer Ishmael Hanes talks about his work

I'm a crime writer, and I get many of my ideas from real events. As you can imagine, reading the daily newspapers takes up most of my morning. If you read about the same thing in more than one newspaper, you often get different points of view, or you find out extra details, which I love searching for. For example, in one paper there was an article about a young woman who had complained about her neighbor's loud music. She said her terrible headaches were due to the noise. In another paper, the neighbor claimed that he didn't know the woman. When the reporter asked him what kind of music he liked, the neighbor replied that he hardly ever listened to music since he had an accident that had damaged his hearing.

More serious articles about thieves or break-ins are what I like reading about the most. My fans ask me, "Don't you feel depressed if you read too many stories like that?" The honest answer is no! My imagination makes me think about all kinds of situations, and my characters meet all kinds of people around the world.

When I was in school, I always knew that I wanted to write, and so my literature teacher told me about an after-school writing club. I used to go once a week, and it gave me a sense of what I wanted to do in the future. I wasn't very confident either, so meeting other young writers really helped me. We could try out ideas, or discuss how our stories might end.

My parents didn't agree with my choice to become an author. They didn't believe I would earn enough in this kind of work. In fact, they wanted me to study economics. Fortunately, my parents are proud of me now, and I certainly don't have any regrets. I'm glad I went to college in the end because I made new friends and developed my abilities. I even won a prize for an interview with a lawyer which was published during my first year.

1 What does Ishmael say he enjoys most about reading newspapers?
- A using his mornings to only read articles
- B getting ideas for his work from articles
- C reading his favorite reporters' articles
- D noticing missing information in similar articles

2 What does Ishmael say about more serious articles?
- A They are what he prefers to read.
- B His fans don't like him reading those kinds of articles.
- C He creates characters from those kinds of crimes.
- D He is amazed when his readers solve the crimes.

3 Ishmael says that he joined a writing club
- A to help other young writers.
- B in order to please his teacher.
- C to practice writing stories.
- D to get some career advice.

4 How does Ishmael feel now?
- A He is happy about his friendships.
- B He still wants to study economics.
- C He is grateful for meeting a lawyer.
- D He regrets not earning enough money.

5 What would be the best introduction to this article?
- A For Ishmael, nothing is more important than his fans or winning prizes.
- B Ishmael describes how his ideas come from everyday stories in the newspapers and online.
- C In this article, Ishmael explains how he chose writing instead of economics.
- D The man behind the popular detective books tells us about his interest in reading, as well as his career choice.

My progress: /5

1 🎧 5.20 **For each question, choose the correct answer.**

1   You will hear two friends talking about a crime drama they watched on TV.
    What did the girl find hard to understand?
    A   the way the story ended
    B   the reason the crime took place
    C   the behavior of one of the characters

2   You will hear two friends talking about jobs.
    What do they both think would be important for them in a job?
    A   getting along with co-workers
    B   being able to travel a lot
    C   earning a high salary

3   You will hear a boy telling his friend about a campground he went to.
    How did he feel when he was there?
    A   annoyed by some of the other visitors
    B   disappointed with the weather
    C   surprised by how good the facilities were

4   You will hear two friends talking about a school project.
    What is the girl doing?
    A   offering to check what her friend has written
    B   explaining where her friend should look for information
    C   suggesting some ideas that her friend could use

5   You will hear a brother and sister talking about making a cake.
    What do they disagree about?
    A   when to do it
    B   what to put in it
    C   who to give it to

6   You will hear a brother and sister talking about
    a shoe store they've just been to.
    The girl left the store without buying
    anything because
    A   the sales clerks were unhelpful.
    B   the prices were too high.
    C   the shoes were the wrong size.

My progress: /6

92   Listening skills

1 Read and write the sentences in direct speech.

Someone took Mrs. Stonesfield's favorite mug at lunchtime today. Who did it?

1   Robert said that he knew and would tell me what happened the next day.

   "I know and I'll tell you what happened tomorrow."

2   Rosie said that she couldn't be the culprit because she hadn't gone into Mrs. Stonefield's classroom that day.

3   Hannah said that she had seen the mug there two hours before.

4   Jaime and Anna said that they were doing their homework then.

5   Mr. Simpson said he didn't have his own mug, and he borrowed a different mug every day.

2 Order the words to make sentences.

1   if I / Rebecca. / They / asked / named / me / was

2   to Mrs. Greene / She / had / the problem. / asked / talked / she / Lucy / if / about

3   him / with / could / us. / if / he / We / math exercise / help / asked / the

4   the music / Tim and Ben / No, / turn / I / ask / could / didn't / if / they / off.

5   asked / had / school. / You / home / if / I / me / to / after / go

3 Order the letters and complete the sentences.

1   The **dlheneai** headline in the newspaper said, "Manchester United wins cup."

2   The **veidecett** _____ **anddeedm** _____ to know the truth. The criminal refused to speak.

3   Jenny **pewderhis** _____ her answer in court. The judge told her to speak up.

4   The head **ortrerep** _____ **gessutedg** _____ I interview the pop star.

5   Timmy is always **tiintuperngr** _____ when his teacher is talking.

6   The **mlincria** _____ **gedrae** _____ with the police officer that he had hidden the money in a stupid place.

4 Match the sentence halves (1–6) to their endings (A–F).

1   Nina claimed

2   We screamed

3   The judge said

4   My mom's a lawyer,

5   I asked the cameraman

6   Martha and I replied

A   when James jumped out from behind the door.

B   she didn't know who committed the crime.

C   not to film the interview.

D   that we didn't know the answer.

E   it was a very serious crime.

F   and she helps people in court.

8 Fantastic flavors

My goal

Mission Complete!

I can talk about meals and dishes, and express preferences. **5**

I can answer questions about how healthy food is. **3**

I can listen and complete a text with specific words. **4**

I can complete a word puzzle with visual prompts. **1**

I can have a conversation and give an account of what was said. **2**

⊛ Diary

What I already know about food and taste …

_____

_____

What I have learned about food and taste …

_____

_____

And I need …

_____

_____

To do this, I will …

_____

_____

So I can …

_____

_____

I want to practice …

_____

_____

1 Find the words and label the pictures.

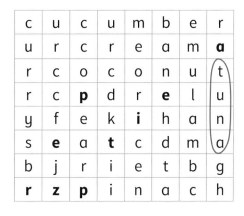
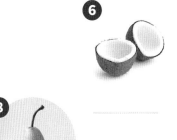

1 — tuna

c	u	c	u	m	b	e	r
u	r	c	r	e	a	m	**a**
r	c	o	c	o	n	u	t
r	c	**p**	d	r	**e**	l	u
y	f	e	k	**i**	h	a	n
s	**e**	a	**t**	c	d	m	a
b	j	r	i	e	t	b	g
r	**z**	**p**	i	n	a	c	h

2 Find the bold letters and write the word. _____

3 Read the descriptions (1–5). Match to the pictures (A–E) and complete the descriptions.

1 No, it isn't vegetarian. It has lots of red, green, and yellow peppers, but there's some ___tuna___ as well. And vegetarians don't eat fish. I think I'll have it for my first course. ☐

2 I choose this one. It's a delicious kind of cake with fruit. Can you guess what the fruit is? It isn't apple, it's _____. I always pour _____ on top. ☐

3 This is Chinese _____, and I always have it when I go to Chinese restaurants. Chicken soup first, then lots of meat, fish like cod, and rice dishes with this on the side. ☐

4 I don't usually like _____, but when I was in Thailand, I tried this! One of the main ingredients is _____, a large white fruit with a shell. ☐

5 That looks nice! There are lots of ingredients, and it's very colorful. What's that in the middle, next to the bread? Is it _____ with _____ on top? I think you can have it before your main course. ☐

A    **B**    **C** 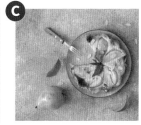   **D** 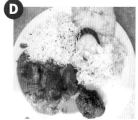   **E**

4 Look at Activity 3 again. In pairs, decide if the dishes are an appetizer, a main course, or a dessert.

> I think the dish of …

The young people below all want to go out for something to eat. Decide which location would be the most suitable for them. For questions 1–4, circle the correct letter (A–F).

1   Maria prefers eating at places that serve breakfast all day. She wants to try somewhere that has recently opened and is popular with young people.

2   James wants to go out with his friends to a place known for its desserts. He'd like somewhere that has special offers and an international selection of desserts to choose from.

3   Niko would like to go out for dinner one evening with her college friends and do some activities while they're there. She'd also like somewhere that offers discounts to students.

4   Michael is going on vacation to India with his family and would like to try a wide range of Indian dishes before he goes abroad. He'd like to find a special event where he can eat outdoors.

Reviews of the city's top places to eat

A

Door to India's food is amazing, and their daily lunch special is one of the best in the city! You get to choose a delicious vegetarian curry with rice and a soft drink for only $10 ($8 for students).

B

Sophie's Kitchen has won many awards for its huge range of delicious sweet dishes by using recipes from around the world. Be sure to download the app to book a table, and get a free drink on your first visit.

C

Come to *1Food* for a food experience that you won't forget! Last year's annual international food festival had over 50 stands selling Brazilian food in the city square. At the same popular location, there'll be even more choice! This year's food sellers are going to be offering typical foods from India such as snacks, desserts, and drinks.

D

At the new *Eat!* festival, you'll try food from around the world. Expect stands to be selling anything from curries from India, to ice cream from Italy. Entry is $2, or free for children under five and students.

E

Joe's is the new favorite place that college students are talking about. This restaurant breaks the rules by offering one menu absolutely full of tasty breakfast, lunch, and dinner dishes served from 9 a.m. till midnight.

F

Make sure you book to eat at *Hot Spot*, or you won't get a table. This popular new restaurant offers the city's tastiest selection of hamburgers, with vegan, vegetarian, and meat versions of every hamburger on the menu. There's an outdoor area to play pool or Ping-Pong for a small fee, or it's free with student ID. Open from noon till late.

⭐ Grammar: reflexive pronouns

1 **Choose the correct answer to complete the sentences.**

1 Did you hurt **yourself** / **herself** when you fell out of the tree?

2 Elena burned **itself** / **herself** on the pizza.

3 I taught **himself** / **myself** to cook.

4 Noa and Emma enjoyed **themselves** / **yourself** at the beach.

5 Ivan cut **ourselves** / **himself** on the steak knife.

6 You and Joel saw **themselves** / **yourselves** on TV after the concert.

2 **Complete the sentences with the correct subject pronoun or reflexive pronoun.**

1 Rachel and Becky, you saw _yourselves_ in the newspaper on the weekend, didn't you?

2 I didn't blame _____ when the vase broke. It was an accident.

3 _____ have to behave yourself when you're in a restaurant, Gabriel.

4 Marta and Carla made _____ go jogging in the park every morning to get in shape.

5 He didn't enjoy _____ last summer. It rained every day.

6 _____ surprised ourselves when our team came first in the competition.

3 **Match the sentence halves (1–6) to their endings (A–F).**

1 James wrote the   A themselves.

2 You cooked the   B ourselves.

3 I'm proud of myself for winning the   C letter himself.

4 We decorated the room   D pasta yourselves.

5 She made the   E art competition.

6 They cleaned up the yard   F bracelet herself.

4 **First ask your friends or family about the following things.** Then, in pairs, ask and share information.

> bake cupcakes   change a lightbulb   do a PowerPoint presentation   make a curry

Lisa, can you make a vegetable curry by yourself?

I'm not sure, I don't think so. I've never tried!

My sister Lucy can't make a vegetable curry by herself.

1 Order the letters to make "food" words.

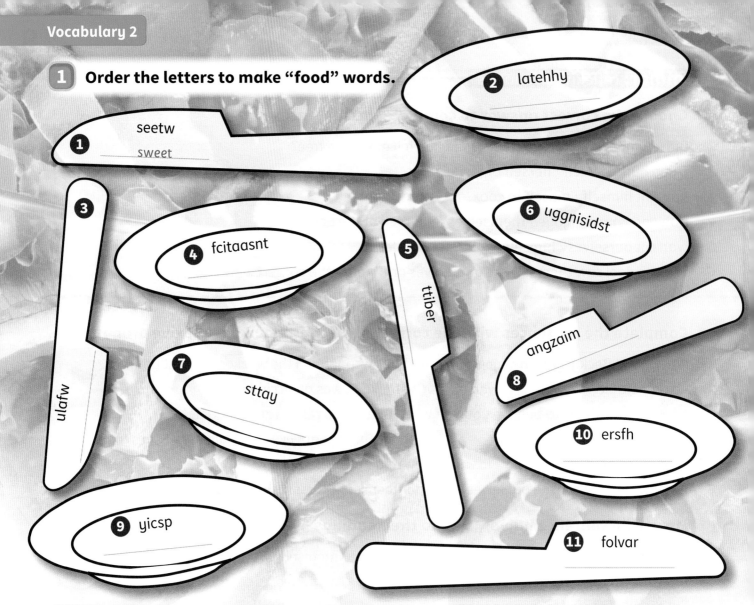

1 seetw
sweet

2 latehhy
_____

3
4 fcitaasnt
_____

ulafw

5 ttiber

6 uggnisidst
_____

7 sttay
_____

8 angzaim
_____

10 ersfh
_____

9 yicsp
_____

11 folvar
_____

2 🎧 5.21 Listen and number the pictures in order.

A   B   C   D

3 🎧 5.22 Listen again and write the words from Activity 1 in the correct column to describe the food in Activity 2.

Person 1	Person 2	Person 3	Person 4

4 Choose the correct answer to complete the sentences.

1 The skin of a fruit like an orange is called **peel** / **top**.

2 The French word for "cotton candy" means **grandpa's** / **dad's** beard.

3 The peppers are called aji peppers because that's the **look** / **sound** people make when they eat them.

4 The boy **can** / **can't** think of one positive thing about his new diet.

8

Grammar: *too* and *enough*

1 **Complete the sentences with *too*, *enough*, *for*, and *to*.**

1 Your dog is ugly, but it isn't ugly ___enough to___ win the World's Ugliest Dog competition.
2 It's _____ late _____ James _____ go out now. It's time for bed!
3 This tea is _____ sweet _____ drink. It has ten sugars in it!
4 Great! It's now only $3. The T-shirt is cheap _____ me _____ buy!
5 Chocolate and candies aren't healthy _____ you _____ eat for lunch in school.
6 Nina doesn't like her pink shoes now. They're _____ small _____ her _____ wear to school.

2 **Complete the sentences with *too*, *enough*, *for*, and *to*.**

 **1** The pencils are _____ big for them _____ use.

 **2** She isn't well _____ go out.

 **3** The lemons are _____ bitter for them _____ eat.

Speaking

3 Watch Pablo and Ezgi do some speaking practice.

Check (✓) the things that Ezgi talks about:

how often she eats out with her family ☐
where her grandparents live ☐
how many cousins she has ☐
what kind of fish she eats ☐
what vegetables she eats ☐
what she enjoys cooking ☐

> **SPEAKING TIP!** Answer the questions with as much information as possible, but don't speak for too long if the teacher wants to ask you another question!

4 **Now plan your answers to the questions.**

Do you like going out for meals?
Who do you like going out with?
Where do you go?
What kind of food do you like?

5 Watch again and (circle) where the stress falls in each question.

1 Do you like going out for meals?
2 Who do you like going out with?
3 Where do you go?
4 What kind of food do you like?

> **PRONUNCIATION TIP!** When talking about things we like, our voice is light and positive. When talking about things we dislike, our voice is flatter and more miserable.

1 **Match the people to the planets.**

1 Lisa   2 Nurse   3 Tilly   4 Temoc

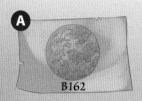 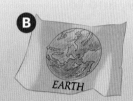  

A B162   B EARTH   C MARS   D Q10

2 **Read the text again. Answer the questions.**

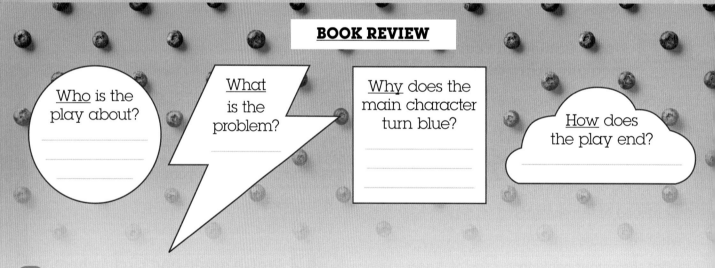

BOOK REVIEW

Who is the play about?
_____
_____
_____

What is the problem?
_____

Why does the main character turn blue?
_____
_____
_____

How does the play end?
_____

3 **Read and complete the text.**

The play is about a young girl named _____Lisa_____ .

One day, she asks her grandfather how to improve her brain power because
_____ , and the school _____ .

Her grandfather says that when he was a boy, they said you should eat lots of
_____ , to improve your brain power.

This gives her an idea, and she eats lots of _____ and
_____ .

Unfortunately, she _____ .

At the end of the play, she _____ and isn't sent back to Q10.

4 ⭐ **Read the text below and choose the correct word for each space.**

Fun facts about food

1 Cutting onions releases a gas … makes you cry.

2 Ketchup was … in the 1830s as a medicine.

3 The fear of vegetables … called lachanophobia.

4 The word "vegetable" has no scientific definition, … you can call a tomato a vegetable.

5 … a lot of beets turns your tongue a pink color.

6 The first … was made from hippopotamus.

7 French fries came from Belgium but are … popular in the U.S.A.

1	A	who	B	which	C	whose	D	when
2	A	drunk	B	eaten	C	made	D	used
3	A	were	B	are	C	is	D	was
4	A	so	B	that	C	but	D	and
5	A	Eat	B	Eaten	C	To eat	D	Eating
6	A	soup	B	snack	C	salad	D	dessert
7	A	a lot	B	more	C	many	D	much

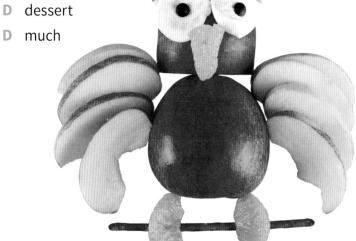

1 **Answer the questions.**

1 What is a healthy diet?

_____

2 Why should we read the labels on prepared food?

_____

3 How much salt is unhealthy?

_____

4 What happens if we eat too much sugar?

_____

5 Why are additives put into food?

_____

2 **Do you always know what you are eating?** Are you sure? Read the ingredients in the candy bar. Can you find the surprise ingredient?

The surprise ingredient is _____.

There may be traces of nuts.

3 **Read the food labels of three different food products at home.** Answer the questions.

Which one contains

1 the most sugar? _____

2 the most fat? _____

3 the most salt and sodium? _____

4 Do any of the food products contain too much sugar, fat, salt, or sodium? _____

4 **Complete the chart with food or meals that contain these ingredients.**

Milk	Cheese, cupcake, chocolate
Eggs	
Wheat	
Nuts	
Fish	
Seafood	

Did you know?

A food allergy is a medical condition that causes you to have a bad reaction to something you eat. The most common food allergies and intolerances are caused by: milk, eggs, wheat, nuts, fish, and seafood. Food additives can also cause allergies.

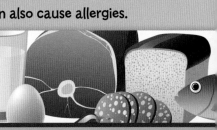
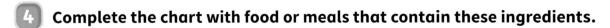

1 🎧 5.23 **For each question, write the correct answer in the blank.** Write one or two words, a number, a date, or a time.

_____

You will hear a man named Rik Price telling a group of young tourists about his work.

Owner of a farm

Rik never has to wear a ¹_____ when he's working.

Rik got some more ²_____ about two years ago.

Rik says that today's menu for the visitors is rice, ³_____ , and a fruit salad.

Rik is very proud of the ⁴_____ that he recently started growing.

Last year, ⁵_____ destroyed all of Rik's peppers.

In next year's Small Farms competition, Rik will need to show how much ⁶_____ the farm does.

My progress: ____ /6

1 **Work in groups of three: one teacher and two students, A and B.**

A and B: listen to the teacher and speak together for 2–3 minutes.

Teacher: ask questions to A <u>or</u> B.

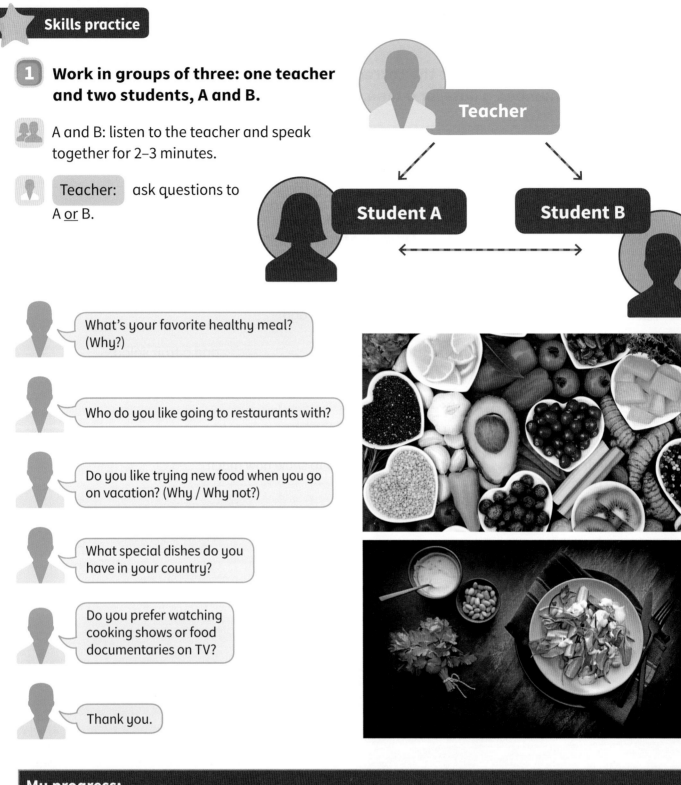

Teacher

Student A ⟷ Student B

What's your favorite healthy meal? (Why?)

Who do you like going to restaurants with?

Do you like trying new food when you go on vacation? (Why / Why not?)

What special dishes do you have in your country?

Do you prefer watching cooking shows or food documentaries on TV?

Thank you.

My progress:		
I understood and answered all the questions. ☐	I understood and answered most of the questions. ☐	I didn't understand all the questions and needed some help. ☐

1 Complete the sentences with the correct reflexive pronouns.

Fiona What did you do last night, Martin?

Martin Andy came to my house and we cooked pizza ¹ __ourselves__ .

Fiona That sounds fun.

Martin Well, no, not really. When I was chopping the onion, I cut ² _____ on a knife.

Fiona Oh, no. What did Andy do?

Martin Well, he ran to get a bandage, but fell over his shoes.

Fiona Did he hurt ³ _____ badly?

Martin Yes, he did. We had to go to the hospital.

Fiona So you didn't enjoy ⁴ _____ last night?

Martin Not really, no. And I'm not going to cook pizza ⁵ _____ again.

2 Match the sentence halves (1–6) to their endings (A–F).

1 You aren't old enough
2 It's too cold for him
3 The bike is too expensive for him
4 Is the lemon cake easy enough for him
5 Are you tired enough
6 The joke is too silly

A to buy.
B to walk to the market by yourself.
C to repeat!
D to go to bed before dinner?
E to go out without a hat and scarf.
F to make himself?

3 Complete the sentences with the words in the box.

| amazing ~~appetizer~~ coconut dessert fantastic main course spicy spinach vegetarian |

When I go out for meals, I always make sure I don't eat too much for the ¹ __appetizer__ or ² _____ , because I want to be able to eat ³ _____ . For me, it's the best part of the meal. I went to a really nice Indian restaurant last weekend for my mom's 40th birthday. They made my mom a special ⁴ _____ cake, which I had with ice cream. I'd never tried it before, but it was ⁵ _____ .

The rest of the meal was ⁶ _____ , too. I don't eat meat or fish, so I always have ⁷ _____ food. We all shared lots of dishes. My favorite was a vegetable curry. It was very hot and ⁸ _____ . When we left the restaurant, my brother said "Aynur, what do you have between your teeth?" When we looked at the pictures of my mom's birthday the next day, there was me smiling with ⁹ _____ between my teeth.

4 In pairs, answer the questions.

1 Think of something you couldn't eat. What was the problem, and what happened?
2 Do you like spicy food? Why / Why not?
3 What aren't you old enough to do yet?
4 What are you too big to do?

> The last thing I really couldn't eat was …

Review ••• Units 7–8

1 Choose the correct answers to complete the sentences.

1 Beth asked Taylor when she **wanted** / **wants** to eat.

2 I asked my sister **cut** / **to cut** my hair.

3 Georgia hurt **her** / **herself** when she fell on the ice.

4 Daniel and Sara said that their appetizers **were** / **are** disappointing.

5 It wasn't good **enough for** / **enough to** win the competition.

6 The meal was **enough** / **too** big for me. My stomach hurts now.

2 Complete the sentences with the correct words.

1 They asked me if I ___would___ take a picture of them.

2 I enjoyed _____ at your party last weekend, Tomás.

3 The judge said that it _____ been an easy decision. Both sides argued the case well.

4 Ben looked at _____ in the picture, and he didn't like how he looked.

3 ⊙ Find the mistake in each sentence. Re-write the sentences correctly.

1 You complained about that restaurant lots of times before.

   You have complained about that restaurant lots of times before.

2 Camila asked me how old am I.

   _____

3 I bought some new clothes for me.

   _____

4 The detective said to me that he asks you a lot of questions.

   _____

5 He said he likes his meal.

   _____

6 I enjoy me a lot when I go to a restaurant.

   _____

3 Complete the sentences with the correct word.

> flavor   fresh   spicy   sweet

I wanted to make a new [1]_____ of ice cream, so I decided to try something [2]_____ like hot pepper. I picked some [3]_____ chili peppers from my yard. I put them on my chocolate ice cream. But I did not like the taste of pepper with [4]_____ chocolate.

1 **Look at the sign below.** Think about your article.

Articles wanted!

Awesome Restaurants

What makes an awesome restaurant?

Is it the kind of food, the staff, the decoration – or all of these things?

How important is it to have a choice of healthy food on the menu?

Tell us what you think!

---

2 **Read Lei's article.** Add the following phrases to persuade: *I don't think it matters, the food should be, it's important that.*

An awesome restaurant is one that gives a warm welcome to everyone in the family. The waiters should be friendly to everyone. I also like it when they're funny. A restaurant doesn't need to have lots of kinds of dishes on the menu – you can't expect paella in a Chinese restaurant, even if it is your favorite meal, but ¹_____ delicious. As for the atmosphere, ²_____ everyone's having fun. It's good if there's a choice of healthy food on the menu, but I eat healthy food at home every day, so ³_____ eating things like cake and ice cream instead of fruit occasionally.

3 **Now answer the question in Activity 1.** Write your article in about 100 words.

You must give good examples to persuade the reader to agree with you.

9 Raining cats and dogs

Mission Complete!

My goal

I can write an email reply to a friend. **5**

I can tell a story using visual aids. **3**

I can read and understand a text about tornadoes. **4**

I can read sentences about about the Earth and say if they are true or false. **1**

I can identify different topics in conversations. **2**

And I need ...

To do this, I will ...

So I can ...

I want to practice ...

Diary

What I already know about the weather ...

What I have learned about the weather ...

9

1 Complete the texts with "weather" words.

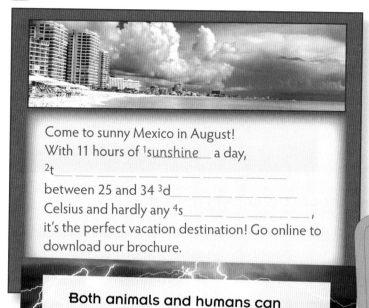

Come to sunny Mexico in August!
With 11 hours of ¹sunshine a day,
²t_ _ _ _ _ _ _ _ _ _ _
between 25 and 34 ³d_ _ _ _ _ _ _ _ _
Celsius and hardly any ⁴s_ _ _ _ _ _ _ _ _ _,
it's the perfect vacation destination! Go online to
download our brochure.

Both animals and humans can
suffer from astraphobia, a fear
of ⁹t_ _ _ _ _ _ _ _ _ _ _ and
¹⁰l_ _ _ _ _ _ _ _ _ _ _ .

Michael Fish presented a
⁵w_ _ _ _ _ _ _ f_ _ _ _ _ _ _ _ in 1987
and told people not to worry about a
⁶s_ _ _ _ _ _ _ . The next day, the worst one
for three centuries hit Southern England!

FACT FILE

When you think of Australia,
you usually think of extreme
⁷h_ _ _ _ _ _ _ and barbecues
at the beach. But in 1900,
Australia had its heaviest ever
⁸s_ _ _ _ _ _ _ _ _ _ _ _ . In
some places, it was 50 cm deep!

This is the Beaufort scale, which is used to
measure wind speed (in kilometers per hour).

2	3	4	5	6	7	8	9
light ¹¹b_ _ _ _ _	gentle	moderate	fresh	strong	near ¹²g_ _ _	fresh	strong
6–11	12–19	20–28	29–38	39–49	50–61	62–74	75–88

2 Complete the chart with what people can do in the weather conditions.

😊		🙁
	sunshine	
	showers	
	storm	
	snowfall	
	thunder	
	lightning	

Welcome to my town!

The weather is usually
great here, but don't
worry if it rains. Here
is our new ten-screen
movie theater. All the
newest movies are
shown here, and the
popcorn is delicious! It's
perfect for when it rains.

3 In pairs, talk about your town/city. Say what you can do in different kinds of weather.

When it rains, you can go to …

1 🎧 5.24 **Listen and ⭕circle the words that you don't hear.**

1 doctor   problem   ⭕snowy   old
2 four   kilometer   seconds   crisp
3 unusual   dark   lucky   tennis
4 rock   windy   cottage   mountains
5 forecast   heavy   thunder   dangerous
6 beach   water   strong   huge

2 🎧 5.25 ⭐ **Listen again. For each question, choose the correct answer.**

1 You will hear a brother and sister talking about their grandfather.

 What do they say about him?

 A   He's good at making people laugh.
 B   He has certain health problems.
 C   He always behaves in the same way.

2 You will hear two friends talking about a storm.

 How does the girl feel?

 A   unsure whether to trust her friend
 B   anxious about what might happen
 C   impressed by her friend's knowledge of lightings

3 You will hear a girl talking to her friend about her day yesterday.

 What was she upset about?

 A   not having the time to do everything she wanted
 B   not feeling warm enough to go out
 C   not being able to do what she'd planned

4 You will hear a girl telling a friend about a vacation she had in Scotland.

 What surprised her about the place she went to?

 A   how much the weather changed
 B   how friendly the local people were
 C   how beautiful the landscape was

5 You will hear a mother and her son talking about the weather tomorrow.

 The boy thinks his mother

 A   worries too much.
 B   needs to be careful.
 C   has the wrong information.

6 You will hear a brother and sister talking about a video they are watching.

 They agree that the man in the video

 A   is doing something dangerous.
 B   is amusing to look at.
 C   is familiar to them.

★ **Grammar:** review first and second conditionals

1 **Choose the correct words to complete the sentences.** Then (circle) 1st or 2nd conditional.

1 We **don't** / (**wouldn't**) wear scarves if it was 40°C! **1st** / (**2nd**)
2 If you **take** / **took** your umbrella, you won't get wet. **1st** / **2nd**
3 I **am** / **'ll be** amazed if there's snowfall in July. **1st** / **2nd**
4 **Would** / **Will** they scream if they hear thunder? **1st** / **2nd**
5 If a snowman **can** / **could** speak, I'd be surprised! **1st** / **2nd**
6 If you **made** / **make** a mistake, would you tell me? **1st** / **2nd**

2 **Match the sentence halves (1–8) to their endings (A–H).**

1 If you forget your homework,   A   they wouldn't wear them in the snow.
2 If Sophia and Aria had new shoes,   B   you would tell everyone!
3 If Rafael was sad,   C   I wouldn't buy him another present.
4 If you don't wear sunglasses,   D   he would talk to Amy.
5 If Sam is on vacation,   E   Mrs. Chang won't be happy.
6 If Marta told you a secret,   F   your eyes will hurt.
7 If you swim in the sea in January,   G   you'll freeze!
8 If James didn't say thank you,   H   he won't come to your party.

3 **Write complete sentences.**

1 I / not call Grandma / she / be upset _____
2 Dad / fly to Berlin / they / not cancel the plane _____
3 your bike / be better / you / enter the bike race _____
4 they / eat ice cream / it / not snowing _____

4 **In pairs, look and complete the sentences.**

If he doesn't eat his vegetables, he'll …

1 If he doesn't eat his vegetables, …
2 … if he doesn't score a goal.
3 If I met a dog that could dance, …
4 … if my parents owned a candy store.

1 **Look and write the complete word.**

1 ☐y☐i☐a☐ <u>typical</u>
2 c☐o☐ _____
3 ☐a☐m _____
4 h☐m☐d _____
5 ☐e☐ _____

6 m☐l☐ _____
7 ☐r☐e☐i☐g _____
8 s☐o☐y _____
9 ☐c☐ _____
10 d☐y _____

2 **Order the words from hot to cold.**

| cool freezing mild warm |

_____   _____   _____   _____

3 5.26 **Take the quiz. Answer _yes_ or _no_. Then listen and check your answers.**

1 The most humid places on Earth, like Kuala Lumpur and Hong Kong, are farthest from the Equator. _____

2 Due to global warming, the mountains in the Alps aren't as snowy now, so ski resorts are using helicopters to drop white powder that looks like snow! _____

3 The wettest place on Earth is Mawsynram, in India. In a typical year, there is 11.87 meters of rainfall. So, imagine you have six tall basketball players, and they stand on each other's shoulders – the water would cover their heads! _____

4 This is a Beluga whale. It is the only whale that stays in the Arctic when the icy water freezes. _____

5 Antofagasta in Chile, which is the driest place on Earth, only gets 1 mm of rain a year! _____

4 **Find three interesting weather facts and write a quiz.**

★ Grammar: *I wish ...*

1 **Complete the sentences with *wish* and the correct form of the verb in the box.**

~~be~~   can   have   let   not have to go   not live

1   I __wish__ it __was__ summer.
2   We _____ our dad _____ in Antarctica.
3   Ahmet and Esma _____ their mom _____ them go to bed later.

4   You _____ you _____ to the dentist today.
5   James _____ he _____ a brother.
6   The cat _____ it _____ fly.

2 **Complete the sentences about the pictures.**

1   Hannah _____ a camel (can ride)

2   Alvaro and Diego _____ superheroes. (be)

3   Ben _____ the correct answer. (know)

Speaking

3 ▶ **Watch Pablo and Ezgi do some speaking practice. Circle the topics they talk about.**

buildings   clothes   dinosaurs   food   movies   shopping   sports   the beach   weather

4 📝 **Discuss the pictures in the video.** Then plan your answers to the questions.

1   Have you ever been to a different city in winter?

2   What do you think students would like to do in your city?

5 ▶ **Watch again and write the tag questions you hear.**

1   There are lots of things to do in capital cities, _____?
2   It looks fun, _____?
3   It looks cold, _____?

SPEAKING TIP!
When you're talking about a picture, try to think of useful ideas and vocabulary about the topic.

PRONUNCIATION TIP!   Try to make your voice go down at the end of a tag question.

1 **Number the pictures in order.**

A

B

C

D

E

4th Annual

PHOTOGRAPHY
COMPETITION

No age limit
All welcome
1st 2nd 3rd Prizes

1

F

2 **In pairs, tell the story from the pictures.**   The three friends wanted to enter the …

3 **Read the story again and complete the sentences.**

1   At first, Mitzi wanted to take _____ *pictures of people working* _____.

2   In the end, they all decided _____.

3   On Friday, James checked _____.

4   Kevin didn't think _____.

5   When they reached the hills, they saw _____.

6   An hour after they started climbing, it _____.

7   They had to climb up to the top of the hill to _____.

8   The police sent _____.

9   Mitzi took a picture of the helicopter and _____.

4 ⭐ **Mitzi, James, and Kevin are looking for new after-school activities.** Below there are descriptions of six different after-school clubs for young people. Decide which club would be the most suitable for each child.

Mitzi loves being in the water, so she'd like to find somewhere she can swim. She is not very competitive and is not interested in getting onto a team. She's also eager to meet new people and have fun.

James enjoys being out in the fresh air, and he loves nature. He's interested in joining a group of young people who like being outdoors, too. He enjoys being active.

Kevin loves being out and about on his bike. He dreams of being a competitive cyclist one day and would love to practice to be the best. He loves being a member of a team, and he loves winning!

A   Nature Trail

This is the ideal place to increase your knowledge of local flora and fauna! We have daily talks and seminars from experts in the field. Once a month, we organize a walk out into the country, so you can test your new knowledge.

B   Youth Club

This is a great club for youngsters who enjoy sports like tennis, soccer, and swimming but are also interested in meeting people of their own age and in enjoying social activities like a once-a-week disco.

C   Free Wheeling

This club gives young people the opportunity to be great cyclists. Learn all the best techniques from other members and share your rides with them. It's all great fun! We also have a gym to help you get in shape!

D   All Sports

What are your favorite sports? Cycling, soccer, table tennis, basketball?

This is a club where you can watch your favorite sports on the large screen. We also have a variety of video games with the theme of sports. Enjoy our social program that includes parties and dancing.

E   Keep Active

This is the club to join if you love sports. We have cycling, tennis, soccer, volleyball, windsurfing, and swimming. We organize competitions in all our sports. Try out for the different teams, and meet our expert coaches.

F   Out And About

This club is perfect for those who love the outdoors. We organize day-long walks out in the hills and enjoy nature. Meet people of your age with the same interests, and stay in shape!

1 Read the text about tornadoes.

Tornadoes form over land. They form when air masses with a big temperature difference meet. The colder air pushes up the warm air very quickly, and this causes the air to start spinning. It forms a dark, spinning column that can travel across the land at 800 kilometers per hour. Tornadoes are sometimes called twisters because of the way they move. They look like big, black thunderclouds with a tail, but they are much more dangerous than a thunderstorm. When the tornado touches the ground, it can destroy everything in its path. It can pull up trees and throw buildings up into the air. It is like an enormous vacuum cleaner! Tornadoes are also very noisy. When they hit the ground, the noise can be as loud as a jumbo jet. Although tornadoes are very dangerous, some people chase them in their cars and try to drive through them for fun. They are called tornado chasers.

2 Complete the chart about tornadoes.

	Tornadoes
Where do they form?	
Why do they form?	
How fast can they move?	
What are their consequences?	
Why do some people go into them?	

3 Find out information about a recent hurricane.

1 What was its name?

_____

2 When did it happen?

_____

3 Which countries did it affect?

_____

4 How many days did it last?

_____

5 What were the consequences of this hurricane?

_____

4 In pairs, discuss what people need after a disaster.

Think about:

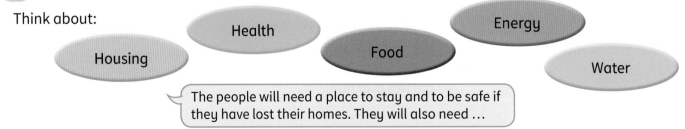

Housing   Health   Food   Energy   Water

The people will need a place to stay and to be safe if they have lost their homes. They will also need …

1 **Read this email from your English-speaking friend, Trea, and the notes you have made.**

To:	
From:	Trea

Hi,

You'll never believe it! I've won two tickets to attend the skiing championships on Saturday! Would you like to go with my family and me? ——————————————————————— Yes, please

The event starts at 10 a.m., so we'll need to leave really early. Can you get to my house by 8 a.m., or do you want us to pick you up on the way to the ski resort? ——— Say which you prefer

After the ski event, we can do a winter sport! Would you prefer to go snowboarding or ice-skating? ——————————— Explain

We're going to be outside most of the day, so don't forget to wear really warm clothes. I have lots of winter clothes. Do you need to borrow anything? ———————————— Ask to borrow

See you!

Trea

Write your email to Trea in about 100 words, using all your notes.

To:	
From:	

_____

_____

_____

_____

_____

_____

_____

_____

My progress: ☐ /5

1 **Work in groups of three: one teacher and two students, A and B.**

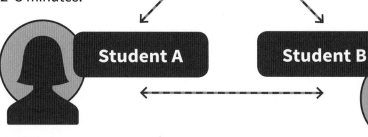
Teacher
Student A
Student B

A and B: close your books. Listen to the teacher and speak together for 2–3 minutes.

Teacher: read and then listen to A and B speak. Use a timer.

> Now, in this part of the speaking practice you're going to talk about something together for about two minutes. I'm going to describe a situation to you.

Show A and B the pictures.

> A teacher is talking to her students about a place for their school party. Here are some places they could go to. Talk together about the different places they could go to, and say which would be best. All right? Now, talk together.

> Thank you.

My progress:

I understood and answered all the questions. ☐	I understood and answered most of the questions. ☐	I didn't understand all the questions and needed some help. ☐

1 Order the words to make sentences.

1 I / a / If / amazed. / met / be / real / I / would / unicorn,

   If I met a real unicorn, I would be amazed.

2 get / thongs, / If / feet / she / wet. / will / wears / her

3 I / you / my / pop / If / you. / won't / balloon, / forgive

4 ice-skating. / icy, / it / If / so / we / go / wasn't / wouldn't

5 sick? / strawberries, / be / we / we / these / If / will / eat

6 a / you / you / outside / do? / would / during / lightning storm, / what / If / were

2 Read the sentences. Write the wishes.

1 My mom and dad are in Berlin.

   I wish my mom and dad weren't in Berlin.

2 James isn't good at tennis.

3 Lucy doesn't have any headphones.

4 Carolina and Camila's little sister takes their clothes.

5 We don't live in a tent.

6 I can't sing well.

3 The words in bold are in the wrong sentences. Re-write the sentences with the correct word.

1 When there's **weather forecast**, we always go to the seaside.

2 You shouldn't stand under a tree when there's **sunshine** and lightning.

3 I watched the **thunder** last night, and it wasn't good news.

4 It isn't hot and **mild** here, it's just dry.

5 Unfortunately, this is **humid** winter weather for Scotland.

6 It isn't too hot, and it isn't too cold. It's nice and **typical** at this time of year.

4 Look at the situations. What do you wish? Write sentences.

1 Your train is five hours late, and it's raining.

2 You're hungry, and you don't have anything to eat.

3 Your friend has a new pet, and you want one, too.

4 Tyler eats your candy but doesn't ask first.

10 Review unit
Units 1–3

1 **Find and (circle) the words.**

bay   bill   bossy   cash
charming   cheap   classical   cliff
disco   DJ   euro   expensive   folk
harbor   intelligent   jazz   opera
port   recording   return
rude   sell   valley

C	L	A	S	S	I	C	A	L	D	J	H
L	R	E	C	O	R	D	I	N	G	P	A
I	U	U	H	P	E	I	B	A	Y	V	R
F	D	R	E	E	T	S	E	L	L	A	B
F	E	O	A	R	U	C	A	S	H	L	O
B	O	Z	P	A	R	O	B	I	L	L	R
O	E	X	P	E	N	S	I	V	E	E	P
S	X	J	A	Z	Z	F	O	L	K	Y	O
S	C	H	A	R	M	I	N	G	P	K	R
Y	I	N	T	E	L	L	I	G	E	N	T

2 **Write words for each topic.** Use words from Activity 1 and Units 1–3.

Personality	World Around Us	Shopping/Money	Music
charming			

3 **Match to make sentences.** Write the letter for the picture.

1 If you keep receipts,   A when you don't have cash.   ☐

2 People who find sales   B you can return things.   [B]

3 Use credit cards   C used in America.   ☐

4 Sales clerks who are nice D help their sales.   ☐

5 Dollars are bills   E can save money.   ☐

4 Unscramble the sentences. Match.

A **B** **C** **D**

1 take / vacations / like / the / scenery / nice. / is / the / beach / People / to / at / where /

_____

2 nationalities. / many / has / Europe / a / continent / which / is / and / cultures

_____

3 driest / and / continent / the / Antarctica / is / which / has / climate. / coldest / the

_____

4 which / Africa, / many / has / languages / is mostly / the / in / cultures. / and / Southern Hemisphere,

_____

5 Read and (circle) the correct answers.

GLOBAL WARMING

During the 21st century, the Earth's temperature may rise a few degrees. Do you know why the Earth is getting warmer? Human activities are causing the Earth's [1]**warming / warm**. The [2]**burning / burn** of oil and coal has led to increasing levels of gas. The gases are trapped, and this results in the heat of the Earth [3]**increasing / having increased**. This [4]**climbing / climb** in temperature has also been having major effects on the landscape of our planet.

[5]**Studying / Study** global warming influences people to plan and try to change things. The Earth's temperature [6]**rising / rised** may cause changes that will affect both our natural landscapes and all forms of life. One example of this is higher temperatures drying out the land. The [7]**dry out / drying out** of farming areas is not good for food production and farmers. Over time, ice in glaciers and icebergs around the poles may melt. The [8]**melting / melt** of ice would add water to oceans and seas. [9]**Risen / Rising** sea levels affects the Earth. Higher sea levels would flood some islands and coastal areas, causing problems for people, plants, and animals.

Did you know that there are over 1,190 coral islands in the Indian Ocean? The [10]**erupting / erupted** of underwater volcanoes formed islands that are known as the Maldives. [11]**Existing / Exist** less than 1.8 meters above sea level puts these islands at risk.

The [12]**surged / surging** of sea levels would easily make the Maldives disappear underwater. As a result, all life forms on these islands, and any other affected coastal areas, would be greatly affected. This [13]**flooding / flooded** is just one of the results of global warming that we need to think about for the future of our planet.

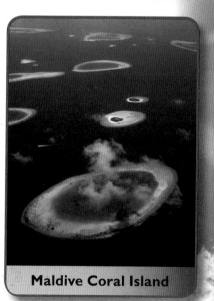

Maldive Coral Island

6 🎧 5.27 Listen and write.

Sam and Tina talk on the phone

Sam: Hi, Tina. What are you doing?

Tina: Hi, Sam. I'm going shopping for my science project, ¹_____ is stressing me out.

Sam: Oh, shopping is my ²_____ favorite thing to do.

Tina: Don't you have to get materials for your project? Shopping isn't my ³_____ favorite activity, but I need things to make my project.

Sam: I have materials left over from other projects that I've done for school. My mom, ⁴_____ is the ⁵_____ organized person ever, filled a backpack with my leftover project materials. I'll probably have ⁶_____ things than you, but I'll be creative and make something cool.

Tina: What are you making? You know the project counts for ⁷_____ than our test grades, right?

Sam: You'll see. It's a surprise ⁸_____ I think will impress you.

Tina: Now I'm curious! I can't wait to see your project, ⁹_____ I just remembered is due this Friday.

Sam: Oh, no. It's due this Friday??? I thought it was due NEXT Friday! I gotta go work on it. Bye!

Tina: Good luck!

7 Complete the sentences using words from the box and your own ideas.

cheap   crowded   expensive   fewer
least   money   most   people   save

1 Buying secondhand clothes is …
cheaper than buying new ones
because you can save money.

2 The most popular store is probably …
_____
_____

3 The store with the …
_____
_____

4 If you exchange the shoes for …
_____
_____

5 The best time to return things is …
_____
_____

8 Write the verbs in the correct form.

Subject: Uh-oh, a party problem!

Dear Ally,

Help! I ¹(don't like think) <u>don't like thinking</u> about my birthday next week. I just want to hang out with my friends on my birthday, but my mom says I can only have three friends over. My problem is that I have more than ten friends, and I ²(keep come up) _____ with more I want to invite! There are exactly 15 on my list. I ³(admit understand) _____ that it isn't fair to ask over more kids than my mom wants, but I ⁴(dislike have) _____ to limit my friends. Whenever my mom asks me about it, I ⁵(avoid talk) _____ to her. Do you have any suggestions?
Thanks in advance!

Sheila

Subject: Re: Uh-oh, a party problem!

Hi Sheila,

It seems like your mom wouldn't ⁶(like have) _____ too many people since you have a small apartment. Maybe you could ⁷_____ (put off celebrate) until the weather is warmer, and we could hang out outside. Do you ⁸(mind wait) _____ and having the party later? It might be good to have more time to plan, and maybe more of your friends would be able to come.

Talk to you later!

Ally

9 Circle the correct verb phrases. Then answer the questions.

1 What does Sheila **want for** / **want to** do for her birthday?
<u>Sheila wants to hang out with her friends on her birthday.</u>

2 How many kids does Sheila's mom **allow her with** / **allow her to** have over?

3 Exactly how many friends does Sheila **wish to** / **wish for** have over?

4 What does Ally **try to** / **try in** suggest as a solution?

5 What would Sheila **need for** / **need to** her birthday celebration to be outdoors?

6 If you were Sheila, would you **prefer to** / **prefer about** postpone the party to have more friends over, or have just a few kids over on your birthday?

Units 4–6

1 **Do the crossword puzzle.** Use words from Units 4–6.

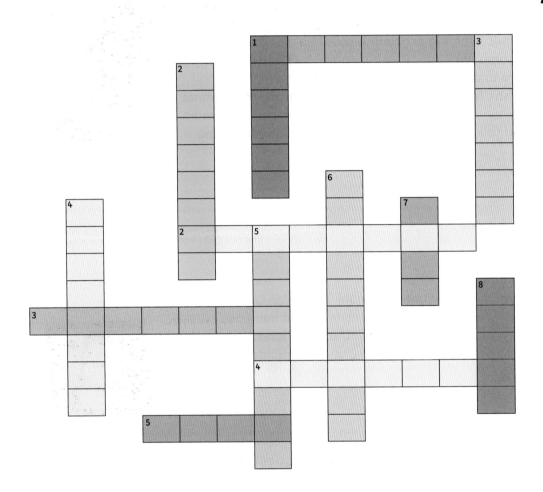

Across

1 This is what you do when you first get to the airport.

_____

2 If a person plays an instrument as a job, he or she is a

_____.

3 When you go on a trip, you bring your clothes in this.

_____

4 An airplane will

_____ from an airport.

5 This person tells employees what to do at a job.

_____

Down

1 The path of your employment is more than a job, it's a _____.

2 When you work all the time, it is _____, not part time.

3 The opposite of feeling calm and confident is feeling _____.

4 If you feel _____, it's a smart idea to ask for help so that you understand.

5 A person who studies science can be called a _____.

6 A person who travels with only a backpack is called a _____.

7 Airplanes do this when they arrive at an airport. _____

8 The people who work at a company are called its _____.

2 Read the messages and fill in the blanks.

| abroad announcement boarding passes check in |
| delay duty-free flight luggage take off passport |

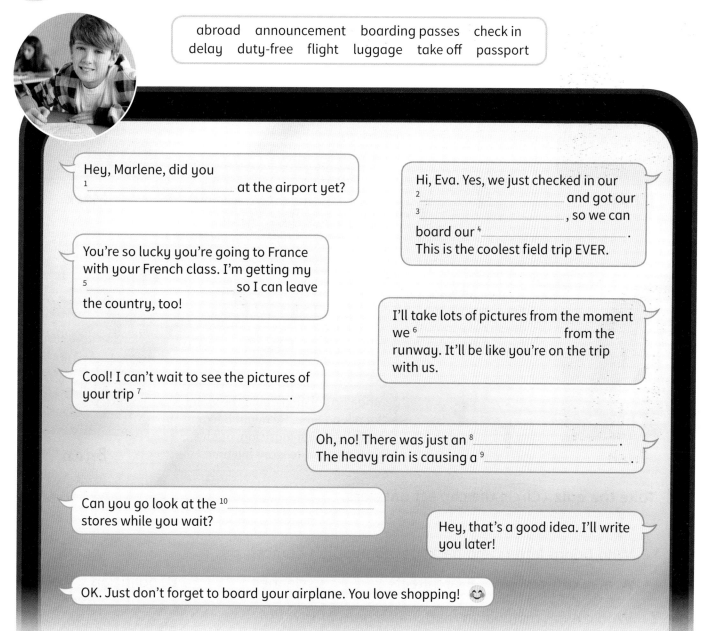

Hey, Marlene, did you
1_____ at the airport yet?

Hi, Eva. Yes, we just checked in our
2_____ and got our
3_____ , so we can
board our 4_____ .
This is the coolest field trip EVER.

You're so lucky you're going to France
with your French class. I'm getting my
5_____ so I can leave
the country, too!

I'll take lots of pictures from the moment
we 6_____ from the
runway. It'll be like you're on the trip
with us.

Cool! I can't wait to see the pictures of
your trip 7_____ .

Oh, no! There was just an 8_____ .
The heavy rain is causing a 9_____ .

Can you go look at the 10_____
stores while you wait?

Hey, that's a good idea. I'll write
you later!

OK. Just don't forget to board your airplane. You love shopping! 😊

3 Look at Activity 2. How do they feel? Circle.

1   Marlene is **disappointed** / **excited** / **jealous** to go on a field trip.

2   Eva is **confused** / **guilty** / **jealous** her friend is going to France.

3   Marlene is **anxious** / **confident** / **delighted** when there is a delay.

4   Eva is **disappointed** / **delighted** / **nervous** Marlene will take many pictures.

4 **Listen and circle T (true) or F (false).**

When they grow up ...

Linda

Linda isn't good at cutting hair. She couldn't be a hairdresser.

T F

Mark

Mark is great at science. He has to be a scientist when he grows up.

T F

Trish

Trish might work part time because she doesn't like to work.

T F

Brian

Brian has been playing the violin for a long time. He might become a professional musician, but he doesn't want to work full time.

T F

5 **Take the quiz. Circle the correct answers.**

1 Who brings letters and packages to people's homes?

    A mail carrier   **B** architect   **C** cleaner   **D** politician

2 Who creates material to read online or in print?

    A programmer   **B** publisher   **C** musician   **D** hairdresser

3 Who sings or uses musical instruments in his or her work?

    A cleaner   **B** hairdresser   **C** scientist   **D** musician

4 Who works in the government?

    A architect   **B** programmer   **C** librarian   **D** politician

5 Who designs houses and buildings?

    A mail carrier   **B** hairdresser   **C** architect   **D** soldier

6 **Play the game.**

Rules

1 Roll the dice to land on a square, and use the words to make a sentence.
2 If you land on purple, write the verb in simple past.
3 If you land on green, write the verb in present perfect.
4 If you land on orange, write the verb in past perfect.

START	1 _____ scientist / listen to hip-hop music	2 _____ student / research information on genes	3 _____ he / get good grades	4 _____ student / write an English essay
5 _____ Karen / work on her science project	6 _____ Jeff / search for evidence	7 _____ he / work at the company for five years	8 _____ publisher / listen to classical music	9 _____ Tom / research information on wild animals
10 _____ we / finish the test	11 _____ she and her sister / work together for three years	12 _____ student / finish the art project	13 _____ Juan / work on his teaching certificate	14 _____ students / write good essays
15 _____ students / take the test	16 _____ mail carrier / listen to folk music	17 _____ the women / be friends for ten years	18 _____ teacher / grade the science projects	**END**

1 Complete the text using words from the box.

> cream   crime   cucumber   Detective   fantastic
> headache   humid   joke   screamed   sunshine

Big brother blues!

Last weekend, my kid brother got sick and ^1_____ at the top of his lungs all morning. Then I got a terrible ^2_____, and my mom told me to go outside. If the weather was nice and there was ^3_____, I could have played soccer. But it was very ^4_____, and between the screams I could hear thunder, so I knew there would be rain showers soon. What could I do?

I tried to ^5_____ to make my brother laugh, but he wouldn't even smile! "He isn't well," said my mom. "He needs to rest. Why don't you help me make lunch?"

"OK," I said, "let's make something nice and healthy like ^6_____ sandwiches." Unfortunately, I put ^7_____ on my sandwich instead of mayonnaise. It was awful, but I ate it!

After lunch, Mom turned the TV on. "Look," she said, "we can watch your favorite show, ^8_____ Lamb. What ^9_____ will he solve today?" About ten minutes later, my brother came downstairs smiling. "Guess what? I feel ^10_____!" he said. I didn't. "What's wrong?" asked mom. "I'm pretty sure it was that sandwich," I said. "Now I feel sick!"

2 Take the quiz. Circle the correct answer.

1   What is a baby sheep called?

   A dessert

   B curry

   C lamb

2   What might you do if you're scared?

   A complain

   B whisper

   C scream

3   What helps clothes dry quickly outside?

   A sunshine

   B thunder

   C pear

4   What is long and green and healthy to eat?

   A coconut

   B cucumber

   C cream

3 Write sentences about each picture.

How was the food?

1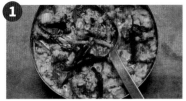

smell / spicy, amazing

The curry smelled spicy and amazing.

2

taste / sweet, delicious

3

look / disappointing, not tasty

4

smell / fresh, sweet

5

taste / too dry, awful

6

smell / fresh, fantastic

4 Write about your experience.

1 What is the most amazing food you've ever eaten?

2 What is the most disappointing meal you've ever had?

3 Have you ever had something too spicy or too sour to eat? What was it?

5 **Complete the text using words from the box and your own phrases.
Then finish the story.**

> breeze   cool   degrees   dry   freezing   gale   heat   humid   icy   lightning
> mild   shower   snowfall   stormy   sunshine   temperature   thunder

SCARY SAILING

My friends Jay and Alex and I decided to sail around the bay. It was Jay's first time sailing, and he said he was nervous. He asked me how long I had been sailing for. He was happy to hear I've been sailing for years. But none of us knew what we were in for that morning.

It was ¹_____ when we got into the boat, but then the sky got dark and ²_____. If you see lightning, then you usually hear thunder a few seconds later. There were loads of ³_____, and suddenly there was silence. "What's going on?" asked Jay nervously. We all studied the sky, which ⁴_____.

If we had known that the weather would become ⁵_____, we never would've gone sailing. Alex said exactly what I was thinking. "If we used our brains, we'd have checked the forecast before we left. This was such a bad idea," he said. Then the weather got scary and ⁶_____. Jay started yelling, and Alex screamed at Jay to stop. I focused on taking care of the boat.

I told Jay, "It looks like the worst is over," but then the boat ⁷_____

_____

_____

_____

_____

And that's our story. That's why we decided to take a break from sailing for the rest of the summer!

6 **Review the story. Circle T (true) or F (false).**

1   Alex said he was nervous about going out on the boat.   T   F

2   The narrator asked how long he had been sailing.   T   F

3   Jay asked what was going on when it got quiet.   T   F

4   Alex said they should have checked the weather forecast.   T   F

7 **Play the game.**

Rules

1 Roll the dice to land on a square.

2 If you land on yellow, write the missing reflexive pronoun to complete the sentence.

3 If you land on green, use the adjective in a sentence *too … to* + infinitive.

4 If you land on blue, say the hypothetical situation using *I wish …*

START	1 Kim ate half the pizza _____.	2 too freezing / go outside	3 Details of the crime were not revealed to reporters, so we had to find out _____.	4 … more sunshine
5 too humid / play soccer	6 … more dessert	7 Jeff came up with a solution to the problem _____.	8 too spicy / taste	9 The students decided to make lunch _____.
10 Tim served us all the curry he made _____.	11 instructions are too confusing / write the essay	12 … more mild days	13 Lucy did the interview _____.	14 too sour / eat
15 … more breezes on our hike	16 We couldn't understand the article _____, so we asked for help.	17 too cold and wet / go swimming	18 … more interesting articles	END

Home Booklet

Paul Drury

CAMBRIDGE
UNIVERSITY PRESS

MUSIC WITH NO MUSIC?

What kind of music do you like: a little pop, some rap, maybe a little classical? Whatever kind of music you like, it makes you feel a certain way. If you're sad, maybe you like to listen to sad music. If you're happy, you listen to happy music. But how would you feel about going to a concert and listening to … nothing? No instruments, no singing – just silence.

This is exactly what the composer John Cage did in 1952. He asked a pianist to go on stage, sit at the piano, raise his hand, and do absolutely nothing. The pianist didn't sing, he didn't dance, he didn't talk, he didn't play a single note. He just sat at the piano.

Why did he do it?

Cage was very serious about his work; it certainly wasn't a joke. Although the piece is often called "Silence", Cage believed that silence didn't exist – there was always something to listen to. He also believed that any sound could be music. He wanted us to pay more attention to the sounds and noises around us.

Why don't you try it?

Sit somewhere comfortable – somewhere that is a little bit dark – and set your stopwatch for one minute (or longer if you can). Get ready and be patient. Close your eyes, open your ears, and just listen. Make a note of everything you hear. How does it make you feel?

Do you think this silent music is strange? Perhaps. But it's an interesting idea, isn't it?

⊛ Home mission

It can be very difficult to find music that everyone likes. Copy the chart below into your notebook and try to find one piece of music that everyone in your family likes. Do you dance to this music?

Name	Style of music	Do you like it?	Name one song / piece of music in this style that you like.
	Classical music		
	Pop music		

WINDOW TO THE WORLD

Japan is famous for being a very modern society, but have you ever heard of Kabuki? This is a traditional kind of opera that can last for around nine hours. You're not excited about the idea? Maybe nine hours is a little long, but you can buy tickets for shorter parts of the performance. It's an amazing experience. It's part play, part opera. The costumes are incredible and the actors are very well trained. Sometimes, the audience calls out the name of the actor. This isn't rude – it's part of the tradition.

Would you like to go to a Kabuki performance? What traditional music or theater do you have in your country? Do you think it would seem unusual to people from other countries?

QUIZATHON!

Guess the answers to these questions. Then match to the answers below.

1 How much did someone pay for the most expensive violin in the world? $_____

2 How tall is the world's biggest drum? _____ meters

3 How heavy is the world's largest bell? _____ kilograms

4 How long is the world's smallest violin? _____ centimeters

5 How old is the oldest instrument ever found? _____ years

> 42,000   6   4.1   16,000,000   202,000

CONFIDENCE BOOST

Some people say I can't sing,
Some people say I can't dance.
That may be true, but I don't care,
I love to sing and I love to dance.
Give me a chance and I won't stop,
Just don't stand too close.

LIVING IN EXTREME CONDITIONS

We humans really are pretty special – we live all over this amazing world of ours in some fairly extreme conditions. We live in some of the highest, wettest, coldest, hottest, and driest parts of the planet. Next time you go out and complain that the weather's not very nice, think about people who live in these places.

The wettest place on Earth where people live: Meghalaya State, India

How wet? Very! It has more rain a year than any other town on the planet: almost 12 meters! For example, a "normal" city like New York has around one meter of rain every year. In Meghalaya, the combination of heat and rain means that lots of structures don't last very long. One solution they have discovered is to make bridges using living tree roots.

This bridge is 500 years old and is made of living tree roots.

Although there's very little rain, there's lots of water in the air.

The driest place on Earth where people live: Arica, Chile (although some people disagree)

Arica has less than one centimeter of rain every year. However, although it has less rain than anywhere else, it's not very dry. Arica sits in a valley, and although it almost never rains, the air is humid. This means that a lot of fruit can grow in the area. The Atacama Desert, which is very close to Arica, is one of the driest places on Earth. In some places there, it hasn't rained for over 500 years.

Would you prefer to live somewhere that is very wet or very dry? Why? What problems do you think people have living in very dry or very wet places?

★ Home mission

Ask everyone at home about the places they've visited. They can be places in your country or abroad.

Find out:

1 what the most beautiful place they've visited is.

2 what the hottest place they've visited is.

3 what the coldest place they've visited is.

4 what the busiest place they've visited is.

WINDOW TO THE WORLD

How many students are there in your school? There are probably more students in your school than people who live in the Vatican City State, which is the world's smallest country. Not only is it the smallest country geographically (0.44 km²), but it also has the smallest population (fewer than 500 people).

Monaco and Nauru are two more very small countries. See if you can find out how small they are and how many people live there.

QUIZATHON!

What do you know about the world's population? Guess the answers and then research the ones you don't know.

1 The population of the world is around 7.6 billion. Which one of these is that number?

7,600,000,000	☐
7,000,600,000	☐
7,600,000	☐
7,000,600	☐

2 A baby is born somewhere in the world about every eight seconds. How many babies are born in an hour?

3 There are more people in China than any other country, but which country has the second biggest population?

4 Which continent has the lowest population?

CONFIDENCE BOOST

So many places to see,
So many things to do.
So many places to be,
Where am I going to?
Take your time, and you will see
What's important to you.

BANKNOTES — MORE THAN JUST PAPER

You go to the store and you want to buy something, so you hand over a bill or some coins. In exchange for the money, the store gives you an ice cream, or a book, or whatever you want to buy. It works because we all trust the bills we use – we know they're real. But have you ever looked at the money you use? I mean, really looked at a banknote? Most banknotes are very high-tech – they have all sorts of ways of preventing copies being made. To you and me, they just feel like a piece of paper or maybe plastic. Here are some of the features that stop bills from being copied.

In this bill, you can see a window and the number ten.

Raised ink: A good way to test a bill is to use your sense of touch, because you can't always trust what your eyes are telling you. This is why many banknotes use a special technique on parts of the bill that make the writing feel bumpy. When you move your finger over the writing, you can feel the bumps.

Holograms: These are amazing pictures that are printed on bills. When you move a bill, the image looks as though it has three dimensions. Also, different colors appear when you move the bill. That's very hard to copy.

Watermark: This is a very common feature, but it's still really special. When you hold up a bill to the light, you can see a picture as if it were inside the bill.

Today, the watermark or hologram is printed in a little plastic window, which is even harder to copy.

Take a look at some of the banknotes from your and other countries. Do they use watermarks or holograms? What pictures do they have?

WINDOW TO THE WORLD

People in many countries are using fewer banknotes and coins, and more things like credit cards and phones to pay. Some people say that Sweden could be the first country to use only plastic money. Of everything that Swedes bought and sold in stores in 2016, only around 1% was paid for using bills or coins.

Do you have a piggy bank? How are you going to save money when there are no notes or coins?

? QUIZATHON!

Here are some questions about money. Guess the answers and then do some research to check.

1 How many countries use the euro? Is it 18, 19, 20, or 21?

2 How many countries use the United States dollar as their main currency? Is it 10, 11, 12, or 13?

3 What is the currency in Japan called? Is it the pen, the yen, or the sen?

4 Which currency has the biggest banknotes? Is it the U.S. dollar, the British pound, or the euro?

5 What is the biggest banknote in your country?

6 How many different sizes of banknotes are there in your country?

CONFIDENCE BOOST

If it's your mom's or your dad's birthday, but your piggy bank is empty,
Think of things you can do that will make them happy – there's plenty.
Clean the house or wash the car,
Do the shopping, but don't go far.
So, give your mom and dad a chair,
Put your coins away,
And show them that you care.

⭐ Home mission

Do you know how much these things cost? Ask everyone in your home and see who's closest. Add two very common foods in your country to the list.

Person's name				
A kilogram of rice				
A loaf of bread				
A liter of milk				

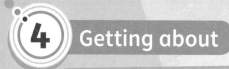

TRAVEL GAMES

You've been stuck in traffic for three hours, and you are bored, bored, bored. What do you do? Do you put on your headphones and look out of the window? Do you just put up with being bored? Well, take off your headphones and try some of these travel games.

I Spy

This is the classic game played by families all over the English-speaking world. One person starts by saying: "I spy with my little eye something beginning with 'c.'" They have to choose something you can all see that begins with that particular letter. Then, all the other players take turns to guess the word: "Is it cow?" "Is it car?" The person who guesses correctly picks the next word.

This is a good game for all ages, but be warned – small children can play this game for hours!

20 Questions

This game is a little like *I Spy*. Think of a thing, a person, or maybe a movie. The other players ask you a maximum of 20 questions to try to guess what it is. But be careful, you can only answer "yes" or "no."

I'm Going to the Store

This is a memory game. The first player starts by saying: "I'm going to the store to buy an apple." The next player says: "I'm going to the store to buy an apple and a banana." The game continues in alphabetical order. It starts easy, but then gets very difficult very quickly.

Spot the Red Car

This is a very, very simple game, which is good, because sometimes, when you're bored, you don't want to think too much. Choose a color or a kind of car, and then see how many you can spot in five minutes. It's surprisingly enjoyable and easy to play.

Silence Game

Maybe your little brother or sister keeps asking: "Are we there yet? How long?" or saying: "I need the bathroom." This game works well, but only for a few minutes. The rule is: try to keep quiet for the longest time. Your challenge is to get other players to break their silence. Try making them laugh by doing something silly.

Do you play any of these games in your country? Which other travel games do you play?

CONFIDENCE BOOST

Nice car, nice bike, nice shoes. It's nice to have something nice.

But it's more important to have something that works.

Home mission

Print or draw a simple map of your city. Put an X where your home is. Ask everyone in your home where they went and how they traveled today. Draw the routes on the map. Who traveled the biggest distance?

QUIZATHON!

Do you think you are very active? Answer these questions to find out.

1   How many steps do you take to go from your front door to your bedroom door?
    Guess: _____
    Actual number: _____

2   How many steps are there from the school gate to your classroom door?
    Guess: _____
    Actual number: _____

3   How many staircases do you walk up on a normal day?
    Guess: _____
    Actual number: _____

4   Do you normally run or walk up the stairs? _____

WINDOW TO THE WORLD

Do you live in a hilly place? Do you have to walk up hills? Have you ever tried to bike up a hill? It's not easy, is it? Well, in Trondheim, in Norway, there is an elevator for bikes. You put your foot on the moving rail, and it carries you and your bike up the hill. Sadly, it's the only one in the world.

Here are two other interesting ways to get around. See what you can find out about:

• the elevated train in Wuppertal, Germany.

• the outdoor escalator in Medellín, Colombia.

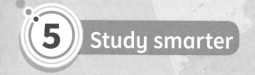

MUSCLE MEMORY

Learning a language, as you know, is not easy. Very often you feel confident until your teacher asks you a question. Suddenly, your eyes open wide, your mouth opens a little, and … nothing comes out. Blank – you've forgotten absolutely everything. You feel confused and very anxious. You don't understand what happened.

Is this what you look like when your teacher asks you a question?

Part of the problem is that you need to develop what is called "muscle memory." When somebody throws a ball, your reaction is to catch it. You do it without thinking: this is muscle memory. This is a skill you started to learn when you were still a baby. It takes time and practice. Remember, you probably dropped the ball hundreds of times before you could catch it.

It's the same when you're learning a language. You need lots and lots of practice.

Here are some top tips:

- Talk to the mirror. The mirror will always wait for you and won't laugh at you if you make a mistake.

- Talk to yourself. The muscles in your mouth need to practice the sounds. It doesn't matter if other people think you're a little strange – you're practicing! Have a conversation – it's all good practice.

- Most importantly, repeat, repeat, repeat.

This sounds a little strange, and you might feel silly, but it really will help. Choose a useful piece of language – for example, *I've eaten …*, *I've never …*, *I've always wanted …*. Think how you can finish the sentences, and say them.

WINDOW TO THE WORLD

Do you complain that you want more homework? Probably not. But if you live in Finland, maybe you do. Research that was carried out a few years ago showed that many children in Finland do less than three hours of homework every week.

What do you think? Would you like less homework? Do you think homework is important?

CONFIDENCE BOOST

The top, the first, the best,
It's good to aim high.
But do you really want to be
Better than the rest?
Isn't it better to be
The best that you can be?

⭐ Home mission

Find out the study habits of everyone at home and complete the chart.

	....	....	....
What are/ were their favorite subjects?			
What is/was their least favorite subject?			
How many hours of homework do/did they do every week?			
Do they have any top study tips?			

Which study tips do you think you could use?

QUIZATHON!

Test your memory. Look at the pictures for 30 seconds, then close your books and write as many as you remember.

THE BEST JOB IN THE WORLD?

Do you know what job you want to do when you're older? Maybe a doctor, a truck driver, an architect, a hairdresser, or a musician? These are all very good jobs. What do they have in common? You need to train, you need experience, you need practice, and you need to work hard. Have you ever thought about what the best job in the world might be?

Look at this picture. What is she doing? She's cuddling a panda – that means she must be a panda carer. Believe it or not, that is a job – all she has to do is spend time with and give lots of love to baby pandas.

Do you want to apply for this job? Well, that's a little harder. You need to be at least 22 years old (sorry, you have to wait a few years) and know about pandas.

Do you know how many people applied for this job? No one's sure, but somewhere around 100,000 people. We clearly like pandas! Is this the best job in the world?

Do you think you would like this job? Why or why not? Do you think this is a real job? Is it hard work?

WINDOW TO THE WORLD

Do you ever order pizza online or on the phone? The pizza delivery person usually arrives by bike or by car, but not if you stay at Jules Undersea Lodge in Florida. Here, if you order pizza, it will be delivered to you by an underwater pizza delivery person. And don't worry – the pizza won't get wet!

Would you like to stay in an underwater hotel? Why or why not?

Would you like to be an underwater pizza delivery person? Why or why not?

Take a look at the jobs and the list of characteristics. Which do you think you need for each job? There's no right or wrong answer, but make sure to give reasons.

Job	Characteristics
Doctor	hard working
	good with people
Engineer	enjoys studying
	enjoys puzzles
Nurse	good listener
	kind
Teacher	patient
	good at drawing
Architect	organized
	good memory

Which characteristics do you have?

🚀 CONFIDENCE BOOST

You still have plenty of time to think about the jobs you want to do.
Architect, cleaner, scientist, or sailor – it's totally up to you!

⭐ Home mission

Talk to everyone at home. Find out how many jobs they've done and whether or not they liked them.

Name	List of jobs	Did they like them? Why / Why not?

Which was their favorite job? Do you want to do the same job?

13

THE HELPFUL BURGLAR

There are many headlines about criminals who make silly mistakes during their crimes. For example, there are lots of stories about thieves who post selfies in the middle of a crime. This gives the police all the information they need to catch the criminal.

What is more unusual is to have a helpful burglar. Normally, a burglar breaks into your home to steal things, but one burglar in England broke in and did the dishes and vacuumed the floors. When the owners of the house returned home after their vacation, they opened the door and discovered a man asleep in one of their beds. He hadn't done any damage, he hadn't stolen anything – in fact, he'd cleaned up the house. He'd also been grocery shopping, made dinner, taken a bath, and washed some clothes.

The couple didn't wake the man up – instead they called the police. When the police arrived, the man was still fast asleep. Reports claim that the man thought nobody lived in the house, and because he needed somewhere to sleep, he broke into the property.

The couple who discovered the thief were shocked, but they weren't scared. They were just happy he hadn't stolen anything.

CONFIDENCE BOOST

It's easy to make mistakes,
It's what we all do.
It's hard to say sorry,
Because that's up to you.

WINDOW TO THE WORLD

Iceland is a large, beautiful island in the North Atlantic Ocean. Just over 330,000 people live there. It's a very peaceful place, with one of the lowest jail populations in the world – around 130 people. Many people live in the country and in small towns, which means neighbors help each other a lot more than in a big city.

How do you help your neighbors? How do your neighbors help you?

QUIZATHON!

Can you solve this puzzle? How does John know that Lucy is lying?

John: Is that my five-dollar bill?

Lucy: No, this is mine. I found it between pages 67 and 68 of my book.

John: You're lying – I can prove it.

⭐ Home mission

Discuss these crimes with your family. Can you think of an unusual punishment for each one?
1 Breaking into people's homes.
2 Stealing people's identities.
3 Cheating in exams.
4 Driving too fast.

THE FUTURE OF FOOD

The world's population is growing quickly. Right now, there are around seven billion people in the world: that's a seven + nine zeros. In the next 50 years, the population is likely to grow to ten billion. Sadly, not everyone has enough to eat, so this kind of population growth means we all need to think differently about food. Here are some ideas to think about.

Growing food in the right places

One part of the problem is getting all those tasty vegetables from the farms to the people who eat them. Think about it – one cucumber is pretty heavy, so 100 cucumbers are very heavy. They all need to be packed into trucks and driven hundreds of kilometers which costs a lot in gas. But now, more and more food is being grown in cities.

Growing food vertically

The main problems in cities are that there's no space and land is very expensive. This means that very soon you might see vertical farms. Instead of growing horizontally, you grow upward, almost like apartments in a building.

Aquaculture

For hundreds of years, farmers have grown certain foods together – what one plant doesn't need, the other uses for energy. This is what happens in aquaponics. The fish make the water dirty, but this dirty water is full of food that helps the plants grow. The plants take the food and grow, and they make the water cleaner, too.

Meat from a test tube

This last one might sound a little strange: meat, not from an animal, but from a laboratory. Does that mean that vegetarians could eat this meat? Would you eat meat from a test tube?

Which do you think is the best idea? Why?

WINDOW TO THE WRLD

What's more important: for food to look good, or for it to taste nice? Or maybe it's a little of both? There is a restaurant in Paris, with branches globally (in London, Melbourne, and Auckland), where you eat your food in complete darkness – you can't see anything. The waiters are all blind, so they have no problem finding you or your table. Would you like to visit this restaurant? Why or why not?

QUIZATHON!

Can you think of a food for every letter of the alphabet? Some letters are very difficult!

a = apple, b = banana ...

CONFIDENCE BOOST

You can't say you don't like it,
Until you've tried it.
Try it once, try it twice,
try it three times.
Just a little.
You know you might like it,
After you've tried it.
Tried it once,
tried it twice,
tried it three times.

⭐ Home mission

Find out what everyone at home thinks about the following questions:

1 Could you live as a vegetarian? Why or why not? (If you are a vegetarian, do you think you could go back to eating meat? Why or why not?)
2 Would you eat meat that was grown in a laboratory? Why or why not?
3 What's the most amazing meal you've ever had?
4 What's the most disappointing meal you've ever had?

IT'S RAINING FROGS AND ALLIGATORS?

We all know what rain is, don't we? Water vapor that condenses, forms a cloud, and then falls from the sky. And, yes, when it rains, this is what happens ... usually. However, there have been reports of some very strange things falling from the sky instead of rain. Here are some examples.

Falling frogs

One day in 1981, in a city in southern Greece, people went out into the streets to find thousands of small frogs falling from the sky. Scientists believe they were picked up in a strong wind and carried to Greece. These frogs lived in North Africa, so they were carried in the clouds for hundreds of kilometers.

Solid squid

Back in 1997, a Korean fisherman was out at sea when suddenly something fell out of the sky and hit him on the head. Believe it or not, it was a frozen squid!

Ali the alligator

A frog is pretty small. It's easy to see how it could be picked up in a storm and then dropped during a shower – but an alligator? Yes, in 1843, in the Southern United States, residents of Charleston left their homes after a storm and came face to face with an alligator that was half a meter long. The local newspaper reported that it was looking a little confused but well.

You may not have seen anything like this, but what's the biggest storm you've seen? Were you scared?

⊛ Home mission

Talk to everyone at home. Tell them they have three wishes for now and the future. Write them here.

Ask them about travel and work. You could also ask them what wishes they have for your future.

	Wish 1	Wish 2	Wish 3
Name			
Name			
Name			
Name			

WINDOW TO THE WORLD

How cold is cold? If you live anywhere close to Yakutsk in the Russian Far East, cold means -50°C – that's minus 50 degrees Celsius. In these temperatures, everything freezes. If you wear glasses, you have to be careful when you take them off, because they could pull off some skin. What is maybe most amazing is that, in these temperatures, schools are still open, and workers on construction sites are still building houses.

What does "cold" mean in your area?

Do you have heating in your home?

Do you prefer it to be very hot or very cold?

There is no need for freezers at the market in Yakutsk.

QUIZATHON!

Guess the answers and then check.

1 **What's the freezing point of pure water?**
-2°C / 0°C / 2°C

2 **What's the freezing point of salt water?**
-2°C / 0°C / 2°C

3 **What's the boiling point of pure water?**
100°C / 200°C / 80°C

4 **If you are on top of a mountain, is the boiling point higher or lower?**

5 **Can it snow when the temperature is above 0°C?**

6 **What's the hottest temperature ever recorded on Earth?** 48°C / 58°C / 68°C

7 **What's the coldest temperature ever recorded on Earth?** -89°C / -99°C / -109°C

8 **What's the normal temperature of the human body?**

9 **What's the name of the metal used in thermometers? Why is it special?**

CONFIDENCE BOOST

It's good to have wishes and dream about what to do,
But there's only one way to make them come true.
Don't wait for the wish to come to you,
Work hard and make it come to you.

Word	Topic	Part of speech	Example sentence	A similar word?
studio	music	noun	Bands record their music in studios.	

CHALLENGE

Say four "music" words that start with the letter "s"!

Word	Topic	Part of speech	Example sentence	A similar word?

CHALLENGE

Say all the countries you know in English in one minute!

Word	Topic	Part of speech	Example sentence	A similar word?

CHALLENGE

Write down all the "money" words you know in English, from the biggest to the smallest in terms of value.

Word	Topic	Part of speech	Example sentence	A similar word?

CHALLENGE

Draw and label a diagram of a passenger's journey through an airport.

Word	Topic	Part of speech	Example sentence	A similar word?

CHALLENGE

Plan an English homework assignment for your classmates, and share it with them. Choose one piece of homework that you're assigned to do, and give it to your classmate to check.

Word	Topic	Part of speech	Example sentence	A similar word?

CHALLENGE

How many new words can you make from the letters in "computer programmer"?

25

Word	Topic	Part of speech	Example sentence	A similar word?

CHALLENGE

Follow the news in an English-speaking country for one week, and share the most interesting things you find out about what's going on there with your classmates.

Word	Topic	Part of speech	Example sentence	A similar word?

CHALLENGE

Group the "food and drinks" words you know by their syllable count. Which word has the most syllables? Compare your words with your classmates.

9

Word	Topic	Part of speech	Example sentence	A similar word?

CHALLENGE

Find out what the weather is like around the world today. Where would you like to be because of the weather, and what would you do there?

	The most important things I learned	What I most want to remember	What I need to learn more about
Unit 1			
Unit 2			
Unit 3			

	The most important things I learned	What I most want to remember	What I need to learn more about
Unit 4			
Unit 5			
Unit 6			

	The most important things I learned	What I most want to remember	What I need to learn more about
Unit 7			
Unit 8			
Unit 9			